KITCHEN
[*Design Guide*]

Meredith. Books
Des Moines, Iowa

Kitchen Design Guide
Contributing Project Managers/Writers: Amber Barz and Jan Walker, Writing and Editing Services, Inc.
Contributing Graphic Designer: Gayle Schadendorf
Associate Design Director: Todd Emerson Hanson
Copy Chief: Terri Fredrickson
Copy Editor: Kevin Cox
Publishing Operations Manager: Karen Schirm
Senior Editor, Asset & Information Management: Phillip Morgan
Edit and Design Production Coordinator: Mary Lee Gavin
Art and Editorial Sourcing Coordinator: Jackie Swartz
Editorial Assistant: Kaye Chabot
Book Production Managers: Pam Kvitne, Marjorie J. Schenkelberg, Mark Weaver
Imaging Center Operator: Jon Pugh
Contributing Copy Editor: Wendy Wetherbee
Contributing Proofreaders: Julia Bardwell, Heidi Johnson, Nancy Ruhling
Cover Photographer: Laurie Black
Contributing Indexer: Stephanie Reymann
Contributing Illustrator: Larry Schlepphorst

Meredith® Books
Editor in Chief: Gregory H. Kayko
Executive Director, Design: Matt Strelecki
Managing Editor: Amy Tincher-Durik
Executive Editor: Benjamin W. Allen
Senior Editor/Group Manager: Vicki L. Ingham
Senior Associate Design Director: Ken Carlson
Marketing Product Manager: Brent Wiersma

Executive Director, Marketing and New Business: Kevin Kacere
Director, Marketing and Publicity: Amy Nichols
Executive Director, Sales: Ken Zagor
Director, Operations: George A. Susral
Director, Production: Douglas M. Johnston
Business Director: Jim Leonard

Senior Vice President: Karla Jeffries
Vice President and General Manager: Douglas J. Guendel

Better Homes and Gardens® **Magazine**
Editor in Chief: Gayle Goodson Butler
Deputy Editor, Home Design: Oma Blaise Ford

Meredith Publishing Group
President: Jack Griffin
Executive Vice President: Doug Olson

Meredith Corporation
Chairman of the Board: William T. Kerr
President and Chief Executive Officer: Stephen M. Lacy

In Memoriam: E.T. Meredith III (1933–2003)

All of us at Meredith® Books are dedicated to providing you with information and ideas to enhance your home. We welcome your comments and suggestions. Write to us at: Meredith Books, Home Decorating and Design Editorial Department, 1716 Locust St., Des Moines, IA 50309-3023.

Page 191 right: Photo courtesy of SieMatic Möbelwerke, Germany.

Contents

KITCHEN
[*Design Guide*]

Creating the kitchen of your dreams—whether you're building a new one or reworking an existing one—makes your home a better fit for your family. *Better Homes and Gardens® Kitchen Design Guide* leads you through the process, from choosing an appropriate layout to lighting the room. Start the kitchen design process by exploring all the ways you can make your kitchen as functional as possible. Chapter 1: "Explore Your Options" explains the various ways you can lay out your kitchen, from activity-based zones to a plan that is most comfortable for people of all ages and abilities. Whether you want to cook for a crowd or make your small space more functional, there is a kitchen layout that will work for you.

To hone in on the look that highlights your tastes and your home's architectural style, peruse Chapter 2:

Contemporary accents blend with traditional style (opposite). Sleek surfaces make the condo kitchen (left) live large.

"Style Influences." From laid-back looks to cozy, contemporary atmospheres, you'll be able to make a style statement that underscores your personality and lifestyle.

Chapter 3: "Plan the Project" steps you through the various ways you can update your space, from a simple, affordable facelift to a major kitchen addition.

Chapter 4: "Cabinetry and Storage" explains everything you've ever wanted to know about selecting cabinetry and personalizing your kitchen storage, including the latest design trends and finish options.

Chapter 5: "Surface Solutions" provides a pictorial review of the most sought-after and trend-setting surfacing options. The armchair tour includes concrete counters and floors, bamboo floors, wood counters, Lavastone counters, slate floors, cork floors, marble backsplashes, and more.

Chapter 6: "Appliances, Sinks, and Faucets" walks you through the process of selecting appliances and fixtures, from choosing fingerprint-free finishes to narrowing down functional requirements.

Chapter 7: "Lighting Your Kitchen" explains the three types of lighting—ambient, task, and accent—and illustrates how light can make your kitchen more comfortable and attractive.

Chapter 8: "Realize Your Dream" provides an overview of the process, from requesting bids to getting the job done on time. Consult Chapter 9: "Resources" for contact information for some of the organizations involved in residential building and remodeling. Learn the definitions of terms you'll use when talking to professionals about your kitchen project. And refer to the professional and source listings for some of the kitchens featured in this book.

Design Experts

Special thanks to the following designers, who graciously contributed time and knowledge to make this book comprehensive.

Mark Adcock, architect, Denver

Carlene Anderson, CKD, Oakland, California

Bonnie Bagley, NKBA, Seattle

Chris Berry, ASID, St. Louis

James Blair and Ian Lawrence, architects, San Diego

Mick De Giulio, kitchen designer, Chicago

Anna Marie DeMayo, kitchen designer, Kansas City, Missouri

Kathleen Donohue, CMKBD, Eugene, Oregon

Diane Ebeling, CKD, Boulder

Regina Garcia, CKD, Allied ASID, Charleston, South Carolina

Richard Gatling, ASID, Coronado, California

Alan Hilsabeck, Jr., CMKBD, ASID, Associate AIA, Dallas

Annie Han, AIA, and Daniel Mihalyo, AIA, Seattle

Mike Kastner, AIA, Des Moines

Dan Keating, kitchen designer, Bellevue, Washington

Richard Landon, CMKBD, Bellevue, Washington

Beth Merrell, kitchen designer, Charlotte

Jackie Naylor, ASID, Atlanta,

Cathy Osika, AIA, Denver

Matthew Rao, CKD, Atlanta

Jeanne Rapone, CKD, Yarmouth, Maine

Debra Toney, AIA, Denver

Rebekah Zaveloff, CKD, Chicago

Designed for two chefs, this kitchen features wide aisles and lots of counterspace.

CHAPTER 1

Explore Your Options

*Knowing the layout choices will help you
make your kitchen as functional as possible.*

Kitchens today are more than just rooms for cooking meals and washing dishes. Most homeowners find that their kitchen has morphed into the central gathering place and must accommodate several activities. This is the room where you are most likely to connect with family and friends, prepare meals, pay bills, do homework, dine in, clean up, arrange flowers, wrap gifts, do crafts, feed pets, and the list goes on.

"More and more people are putting their design emphasis into the kitchen," says Chicago designer Rebekah Zaveloff. "It has to perform multiple uses for varying groups of people. It's all about creating a room that draws people in and makes it easy for you to spend quality time with family and friends."

Adaptive yet unobtrusive features make the kitchen (opposite) accommodating to people of all ages and abilities. A bar-height peninsula (left) provides workspace for two cooks and enables guests to keep an eye on what's cooking.

ACTIVITY CENTERS

An activity-based kitchen, also referred to as a zoned kitchen, produces the ultimate in comfort and efficiency because it meets every family member's individual needs.

A zoned kitchen, like every well-designed kitchen, starts with a basic work triangle, which is the path between the refrigerator, sink, and cooktop. The goal is to keep this path uninterrupted by traffic or cabinetry and to minimize steps between these components.

Zoned kitchens take this triangular concept a few steps further by connecting three or four additional activity centers to the work area. To illustrate this point, imagine a secondary triangle overlaying the first to minimize steps between a beverage center, a microwave, and a snack bar. To plan your own zoned space, think about the activities that commonly take place in your kitchen and plot your layout accordingly.

This kitchen features restaurant-style efficiency yet is inviting and comfortable for a busy family. "At 16×26 feet, this is a fairly large kitchen, but due to a sequential layout, you never have to move more than 3 feet in any direction to get what you need," explains kitchen designer Alan Hilsabeck, Jr. The floor plan on page 15 shows where each of the kitchen's six zones—preparation, cooking, serving, beverage, baking, and cleanup—is located.

Prep zone

The preparation zone, where meals start, stretches the length of the kitchen, sharing a corridor with the parallel island-based cooking zone. "The concept is the same as that of an assembly line," Hilsabeck explains. "Those doing the prep work can turn around and hand over their work to those doing the actual cooking."

This preparation zone features a long countertop workspace and plentiful storage for small appliances, knives, and ingredients.

At 16×26 feet, this is a fairly large kitchen, but due to a sequential layout, you never have to move more than 3 feet in any direction.

–ALAN HILSABECK, JR., kitchen designer

Beverage zone

The beverage zone enables family members and guests to grab a glass, ice, and something to drink in one convenient location without getting in the cook's way. Customize your beverage center to include the equipment required to make your favorite drink, whether it's a cup of hot brew, a fruit smoothie, or a cold ready-made drink.

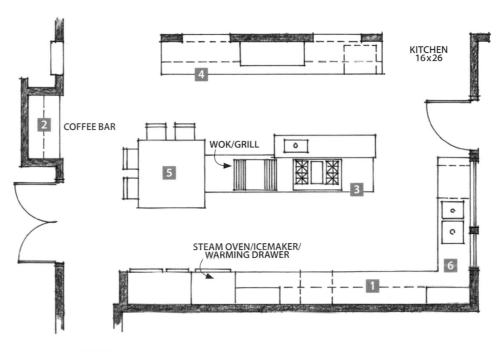

KITCHEN
16x26

COFFEE BAR

WOK/GRILL

STEAM OVEN/ICEMAKER/
WARMING DRAWER

ACTIVITY CENTERS
1. Preparation
2. Beverage
3. Cooking
4. Baking
5. Serving
6. Cleanup

This beverage center is sensibly positioned midway between the refrigerator and dining room—and steps from a wine cellar. The center features a coffee bar with a direct water line. Cups and glasses are within easy reach behind glass-front cabinet doors.

Cooking zone

The cooking zone is the epicenter of the kitchen and should include a cooktop, storage for pots and pans, and a place to stash spices that you add during heating. This island-based zone features two cooktops—one with a wok and griddle (below) and one with four gas burners.

The wok (above) features a precision flame typically found in fine restaurants. On the island's top tier (above right), a sink is handy for rinsing produce or—when filled with ice—chilling Champagne. A cutting board next to the cooktop (right) makes it easy to add last-minute ingredients.

In lieu of a view-blocking hood, each cooktop has a pop-up ventilation system.

Baking zone

A step-saving baking center includes at least a 3-foot-long section of cool stone countertop for rolling out pastry, electrical outlets for operating mixers and food processors, an appliance garage, and additional storage for dry goods such as flour, sugar, and baking soda.

Design Tip

To maximize storage measure the height of the tallest item you will be storing in the space and allow just enough clearance between shelves for it to fit.

In the baking center (above) a counter-to-ceiling cabinet stores flours, sugars, and specialty items while shallow drawers cradle spice bottles. A built-in scale (above left) is convenient for weighing ingredients.

The counter-to-ceiling cabinet that houses the baking center stands between two pass-throughs that open to the dining room. A 20-foot-long countertop provides ample room for rolling out pastry.

Serving zone

If your family is constantly on the go, a serving zone may be a good addition to your plan. This area enables the cook to fill plates for diners to pick up, eliminating the need for serving platters and reducing cleanup time.

A wood slab at one end of the island (above and opposite) is where family and guests pick up plates filled with today's entrée, much as a restaurant server picks up plates at a diner window. The area also serves as a snack bar.

Cleanup zone

This cleanup zone includes a dishwasher, a larger stainless-steel sink, and a high-arc faucet with a restaurant-style sprayer—good choices for any cleanup area. If you entertain a lot, consider a second dishwasher on the opposite side of the sink or near the dining area you use the most.

Dish drawers—smaller dishwashers that take up less cabinet space—are another convenient option, particularly if your cleanup needs change significantly on a regular basis.

The dishwasher (above) is undetectable behind a cabinetry panel that looks like a stack of drawers. Oak planks warm the kitchen floor. A view of a backyard herb garden makes doing dishes feel like less of a chore (right). The preparation zone (opposite) is located next to the cleanup zone so utensils and bowls can be easily transferred to the sink after use.

ISLAND ZONES

A kitchen carefully planned as a series of zones reduces morning chaos. The key to this smooth-running work core is designated stations that centralize food preparation and after-breakfast cleanups.

Breakfast star

This efficient zoned design features two islands that form two distinct areas: one for making breakfast and another for cooking the rest of the day's meals.

The floor plan (see page 30) shows where each of the kitchen's eight zones—desk, mail sorting, gift wrapping, message center, mudroom storage, breakfast station, island banquette, and cooking—is located.

In this breakfast station (right), certified master kitchen and bath designer Jackie Naylor incorporated a coffee spot (above). Providing a niche for the appliance as well as coffee and sugar canisters keeps the front of the counter clear for mugs and other necessities.

A kitchen design that focuses on specific zones helps contain the clutter and saves steps when you're trying to fix breakfast or wash dishes.

— JACKIE NAYLOR, kitchen designer

Efficient cooking

When designing a cooking zone for your kitchen, work in plenty of counterspace for preparing foods as well as enough storage for pots, pans, and utensils. This cooking center lines one entire wall and culminates with the refrigerator for easy access to cold ingredients. Deep drawers are ideal for your tallest stockpots. Shallow drawers should feature dividers for organizing spices, knives, and other utensils.

Equipped to Cook

The main ingredients of the cooking center are the cooktop or range and the microwave oven. Be sure your cooking center has ample storage for the tools of the cooking trade: pots and pans, utensils, pot holders, hot pads, spices and seasonings, and food products that go directly from the storage container into the simmering pot.

A cooktop is safest and most efficient with at least 18 inches of counterspace on each side. This enables you to turn handles away from traffic and provides a landing space for hot pots and pans. Use a heat-resistant countertop surface around the cooktop or range.

Whether you have a cooktop or a range, the cooking center requires a ventilation system. The number of Btus put off by your cooktop will determine the requirements of your ventilation system. A standard four-burner residential range requires a ventilation system that blows a minimum of 150 cubic feet of air per minute. Professional-style cooktops and ranges typically require more ventilation.

For noon and evening meals, this at-the-ready cooking zone includes a textured stainless-steel backsplash equipped with sleek built-in shelves that can store mixing bowls and other cooking and baking needs.

Quick cleanups

"A kitchen design that focuses on specific zones helps contain the clutter and saves steps when you're trying to fix breakfast or wash dishes," says Jackie Naylor, the designer of this kitchen. The breakfast station features a cleanup zone that makes it easy to clear away cereal bowls and juice glasses after the morning meal. A snack bar with stools parallels the breakfast and cleanup zones for easy access.

Design Tip

If you have a large space for laying out your kitchen (this one measures about 12×15 feet), consider fitting in two islands. The key to efficiency is to allow at least 36 inches for aisles (42 inches is better). Equip the islands to accommodate specific activities that suit your lifestyle: If you bake, for example, equip an island with a flip-up shelf for a mixer and include a sink. Locate the island across from a double oven.

The small undermount sink in the breakfast bar (left) accommodates rinsing dishware and preparing vegetables and fruits but doesn't consume precious counterspace. A set of dishwasher drawers to the right of the sink is ideal for small loads. Refrigerator drawers to the left of the sink keep beverages and produce close at hand. A family dining spot (opposite) nestles up to the back of the snack bar island to make the most of floor space. The banquette offers an abundance of seating as well as roomy storage drawers under the bench seats.

Clutter busters

To prevent your kitchen island from becoming the catch-all for book bags and sports gear, create an adjacent mudroom storage zone. The mudroom adjoining this kitchen offers several efficient zones: The built-in desk provides a place to plan meals, do homework, and pay bills. A specially outfitted closet serves as a gift-wrapping station while another wall holds shelves and a bench for corralling shoes and book bags.

Roll-out trays (left) stow gift wrap; the top tray doubles as a work surface. Dowels keep ribbon tidy. A desk (right) near the kitchen organizes paperwork. For back-door storage (opposite), compartments flank a built-in bench that's an ideal spot to sit and take off shoes or boots.

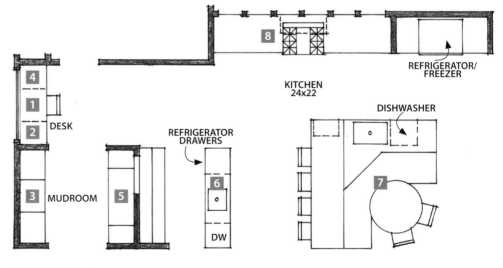

ISLAND ZONES

1. Desk
2. Mail-sorting center
3. Gift-wrapping center
4. Message center
5. Mudroom storage
(cubbies and bench)
6. Breakfast station
7. Island banquette
8. Cooking zone

THEATER STYLE

If you love to cook for a crowd, a theater-style layout may be the right floor plan for you. Theater-style kitchens, where guests gather around as the chef prepares meals, are extremely popular and appeal to people who enjoy entertaining, including kitchen designer Rebekah Zaveloff. Zaveloff is the owner and designer of this compact kitchen.

Use chalkboard paint and molding (right) to turn a door into a message center. Connect a remodeled room to its roots by adding a few antiques, such as a wall-hung spice cabinet (below).

To create a theater effect, Zaveloff simply adds a long bar-height peninsula to accommodate food preparation and control traffic, as she did in this kitchen. Alternatively she uses a long work island with seating on one side.

"Seating along one side enables guests to socialize with the cook while keeping an eye on what's cooking," Zaveloff explains. When more guests are present, Zaveloff pulls up chairs on all three sides of the peninsula.

Design Tip

Contemporary appliances and cabinetry can work well in an older home. To meld the new with the old, pay homage to the existing architecture by matching window moldings and baseboards to those used in other rooms in the home. For more tips on pulling together an eclectic-style kitchen, see pages 98-101.

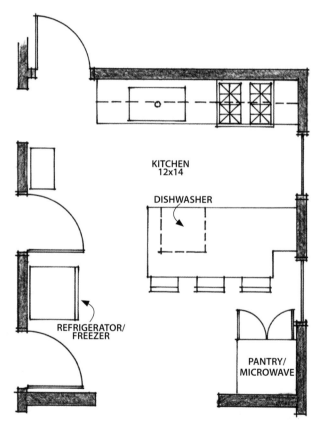

KITCHEN
12x14

DISHWASHER

REFRIGERATOR/
FREEZER

PANTRY/
MICROWAVE

To save money kitchen designer Rebekah Zaveloff suggests purchasing floor models and shopping clearance sales. She gave second life to a sink with a minor flaw and a range hood with exposed rivets (above), both items left over from clients' projects. By mixing tonal colors and textures, she gave her kitchen (opposite) a personal look.

CROWD CONTROL
In this theater-style layout a peninsula separates the work area from the gathering space.

To keep remodeling costs in check, Zaveloff recommends working within the existing walls whenever possible. Adding a peninsula to her own kitchen preserved the doorways, windows, and plumbing lines, allowing the majority of the remodeling budget to be spent on cabinetry, appliances, and surface updates.

Surface choices

To make a small room feel more spacious, choose pale-color cabinets, such as the maple cabinets featured, and add glass inserts to as many upper cabinets as practical. Laminated glass insets, like the ones shown on page 37, reflect light and alleviate the need for neatness.

Choose pale or light-reflecting surfaces that are both easy-care and in line with your personal style. Traditional, salvaged marble covers the perimeter countertops, while trendy concrete tops the island. A glass mosaic tile backsplash and sleek slate floor tiles combine with a subway-tile-covered island base to bring texture and pattern interest.

To add storage for little expense, Zaveloff recommends installing open shelves and racks in the backsplash area (left). These stainless-steel organizers free up drawer space for less attractive fare. "In a small kitchen like this, maximizing the use of every inch of space is necessary," Zaveloff explains. The tall pantry cabinet (opposite) was custom-made to fit in the corner. The cabinet also houses the microwave.

PARTY PLACE

If your kitchen plays host to daily gatherings of family and friends, plan your space so that everyone feels welcome. A backyard addition doubled the size of this kitchen and provides enough seating for a crowd. The modified galley layout, envisioned by kitchen designer Jeanne Rapone, incorporates a spacious island, an eating area, a bar, and wide traffic lanes, creating a venue well suited for entertaining. The curve-top island holds the main sink and two dishwashers and comfortably seats three, while the adjacent table can accommodate eight more.

CONTINUED ON PAGE 42

Pendent fixtures light the granite-top island (left). Breakfast and desserts are often served from this attractive built-in buffet (below).

An Entertaining Plan

The right kitchen layout can help make any get-together a success, whether you're hosting a holiday party for 20 or a dinner for four.

Wide aisles. If you have the space, bump your kitchen's aisle width to 48 inches. The floor space makes it comfortable to work with more than one cook and provides enough width for wheelchairs and walkers.

Cooking capacity. To generate enough oven capacity to cook for a crowd, include at least two conventional ovens, a microwave, and a warming drawer.

Work area. A large center island, such as this 8-foot-long workhorse, provides enough workspace for several cooks and guests to gather. Two sinks—a deep farm-style sink in the island and a smaller one in the beverage center—allow for two cooks to prepare foods or rinse dishes at the same time.

Cleanup zone. To increase a kitchen's cleanup capacity, include two dishwashers. In this kitchen two full-size dishwashers flank the island sink.

Storage capacity. If space allows, you'll also want to include a large pantry cabinet or closet so that you can store lots of cooking supplies, foodstuffs, and serving pieces close at hand.

Ample floor space between the island and perimeter cabinets makes room for multiple cooks and for guests who like to mingle, taste, or pitch in. The pairs of French doors that connect to the patio encourage traffic flow from inside to outdoors.

"The layout is ideal for entertaining because it provides lots of seating for guests, and the aisles are wide enough for people to pass through without getting in the way of the cook," Rapone explains.

Social center

If space allows, Rapone suggests adding a well-stocked beverage center, complete with a sink and a small refrigerator or icemaker. Behind the island seating area in this kitchen, a bar with its own small sink and wine cooler enables guests to help themselves to beverages. Across from one end of the dining table, a built-in hutch offers buffet service.

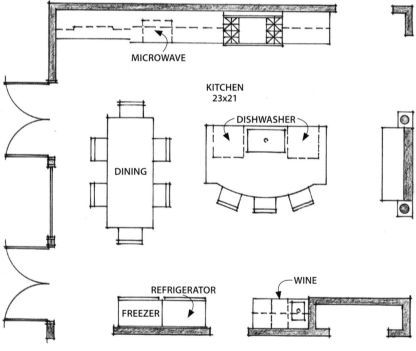

ENTERTAINING PLAN
With multiple seating areas, two dishwashers, two sinks, and a beverage center, this kitchen easily accommodates a crowd.

Glass-front storage cupboards in the beverage center make it easy for guests to help themselves.

The professional-grade range is equipped with two ovens. A few steps away an undercounter microwave facilitates last-minute warming of casseroles or sauces.

KITCHEN LIVING

Opening the dining room (left) to the kitchen makes this space multifunctional, spacious, and light-filled. Dining tables require task lighting, and it needn't be run-of-the-mill. This fixture (below) was assembled using various lamp parts.

Two common complaints about older kitchen layouts are that the space is too dark and too cramped. Removing walls to create an open, loftlike setting helped relieve this kitchen of both troubles. Incorporating translucent glass walls into the design ensures that even more light can filter in from adjoining rooms. "Our goal was to make the rooms feel more spacious," says kitchen designer Annie Han, who designed the space with Daniel Mihalyo. "We proposed building some of the walls from recycled and antique glass to allow light to flow between spaces."

Angling the kitchen peninsula into the dining room brings the cook into the social scene. Side-by-side tables—one surrounded on three sides by banquette seating—create plenty of flexible dining space for entertaining and large family gatherings. The banquette also stands in as a comfortable "sectional" sofa where a large group could linger for hours.

Equipping the banquette area (above) with a low table allows this space to accommodate casual conversation as well as dining. The table height is ideal for serving children's meals.

Rather than sequester the kitchen dining space with solid walls, a bank of cabinetry—topped with a translucent glass divider—defines the space. See-through cabinetry (opposite) mounted on translucent panels admits light along the refrigerator wall as well.

When opening a kitchen to adjacent rooms, locate the cooktop or range as well as the sink for socializing.

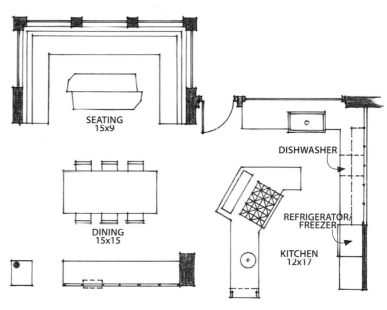

SEATING
15x9

DISHWASHER

DINING
15x15

REFRIGERATOR/
FREEZER

KITCHEN
12x17

KITCHEN LIVING
An L-shape floor plan
allows dual seating areas,
ensuring that a crowd can
gather comfortably.

Positioning the range within the angled peninsula ensures that the cook never feels cut off from the crowd. As the floor plan (above) shows, the range overlooks the dining area and affords a view to the outdoors.

Design Tip

An experienced architect or qualified remodeling contractor can tell you whether a wall you want to remove between your kitchen and adjoining rooms is load-bearing. (A load-bearing wall supports the weight of structures above it. A non-load-bearing structure is called a partition wall.) You can also do some sleuthing yourself in the basement or attic: Check exposed joists or rafters. If these structural members run parallel to the wall in question, it's not a load-bearing wall. However, if the joists or rafters run perpendicular to the wall, you can be reasonably sure that the wall is bearing a load. If the wall is load-bearing, a ceiling beam can be positioned in its place to support the load above.

A second sink is a good idea in even a small kitchen. This sink (opposite) creates a handy station for preparing vegetables or for making beverages. The steel and glass display shelves show off colorful glassware.

Another steel and glass shelf (above) rises behind the range to squeeze more storage and display into this layout. The translucent glass also helps shield kitchen messes from the dining area. Elevated shelf designs such as this one are also useful when located behind a sink. For cleanup, the farmhouse sink (left) features a single-spout faucet with a pullout sprayer. For more convenience, the floor plan provides an unencumbered pathway from the dining table to this sink.

TWO-COOK KITCHEN

If you love to cook, follow the remodeling recipe of this kitchen designed for two professional chefs.

To create volume, kitchen designer Dan Keating tore down the interior walls that separated the kitchen from the living and dining areas and raised the ceiling by eliminating the attic space above. An L-shape island anchors the new great-room and occupies the space once devoted to a laundry/utility area. New windows and skylights increase natural light and draw the entire family to the room.

Design Tip

To ensure that an industrial-strength kitchen doesn't feel cold and austere, choose warm colors and tactile woods. Here Tuscan yellow subway tiles and walls and rich burgundy cabinets add mellow seasoning to the hardworking space.

A deep basin in the sink (left) holds large pots and corrals messes until cleanup time. The island eating area (above) is defined by a glossy oval of solid-surfacing, while the rest of the counters are a durable composite made from restaurant cutting boards. The L-shape island (opposite) also provides space for food preparation and buffet service.

If you want to accommodate two cooks, kitchen designer Bonnie Bagley recommends incorporating multiple cooking and work zones as well as plenty of uninterrupted counterspace. Two sinks and extra-wide aisles ensure a continuous workflow.

High-performance appliances are also a must. This kitchen is equipped with a 48-inch range and a commercial-grade wok that share a 7-foot-wide vent hood. Other restaurant-worthy amenities include a built-in garbage chute, dual dishwashers (one by each sink), and commercial-grade countertops made from resin-infused paper-base laminate.

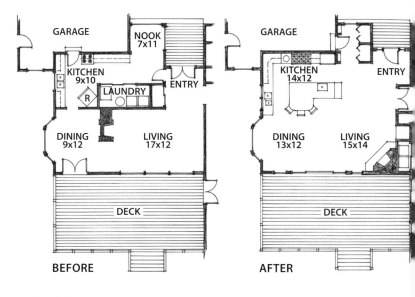

BEFORE   AFTER

TWO-COOK KITCHEN
Wide aisles, professional
appliances, and ample
workspace accommodate
two chefs.

Attractive baskets (above left) keep the countertops clear of clutter. This towel bar (center left) is recessed into the prep side of the island and is easily accessible from either sink. Extra insulation and wider clearances were required for the wok (left), which generates 125,000 Btus (as opposed to the 30,000 Btus of a typical residential wok burner).

If two or more people will be cooking in your kitchen at the same time, plan aisles that are at least 42 inches wide, so that cooks can easily pass one another and there are no clearance issues when appliance doors are open.

An island is a kid-friendly feature. Stools (left) pull up to the countertop so kids can converse with parents or work on a project.

FAMILY FOCUSED

Whether you build new or remodel, your family may grow after you've moved in. If that's the case, your kitchen may need a kid-friendly makeover similar to this one. Architect Cathy Osika came on the scene to help the family of five gain the kitchen function they needed without sacrificing the charm of their historical home. They also requested the kind of open, airy spaces commonly found in urban lofts.

Classic moldings (above) ease the transition between the kitchen addition and the historical house.

An addition, plus merging the kitchen with adjacent spaces, yielded the square footage needed to make the kitchen family-efficient. Although this kind of open planning allows easy gathering, it can also yield a boring, boxy look. To avoid that syndrome Osika separated areas with built-ins rather than with walls and then added volume-enhancing windows and French doors.

Design Tip

When you know your kitchen will receive lots of wear from active kids, select durable surfaces that clean up easily. Turn to page 154 to learn more about a wide range of smart options.

An appliance garage (above) stores the gadgets needed for a family kitchen—maltmaker, toaster, and coffee pot.

Backsplashes can be as hardworking as they are beautiful—a huge benefit if you do a lot of cooking for a family. This range (above) boasts an elegant Azul Mare marble backsplash that can be wiped clean.

An undermount sink simplifies cleanup—sweep water and debris from the counter straight into the sink bowl.

For the way the family lives and entertains, establishing activity areas within the room allows each member to be doing something different yet still be in the same room. For example, a desk allows someone to listen to music on the computer or pay bills. When planning a desk area for your kitchen, consider allowing enough counterspace for spreading out books while leaving enough room for the computer. Create a hiding place for unsightly peripherals, such as the printer and wireless modem. The desk area abuts a built-in banquette for family dining, but the table is also a perfect place for doing homework or crafts projects. A generous island with a pair of stools provides a spot for the kids to chat with Mom and Dad while snacking.

Plenty of cold storage is a must in a family kitchen. A built-in refrigerator such as this one (above) provides ample cool cubic feet without encroaching on the floor space. In this old house a niche (opposite) for the radiator gains function with the addition of cabinetry that gives the microwave a built-in look at a useful height.

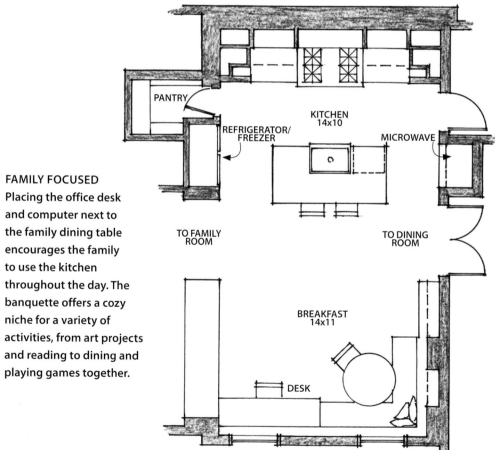

FAMILY FOCUSED
Placing the office desk and computer next to the family dining table encourages the family to use the kitchen throughout the day. The banquette offers a cozy niche for a variety of activities, from art projects and reading to dining and playing games together.

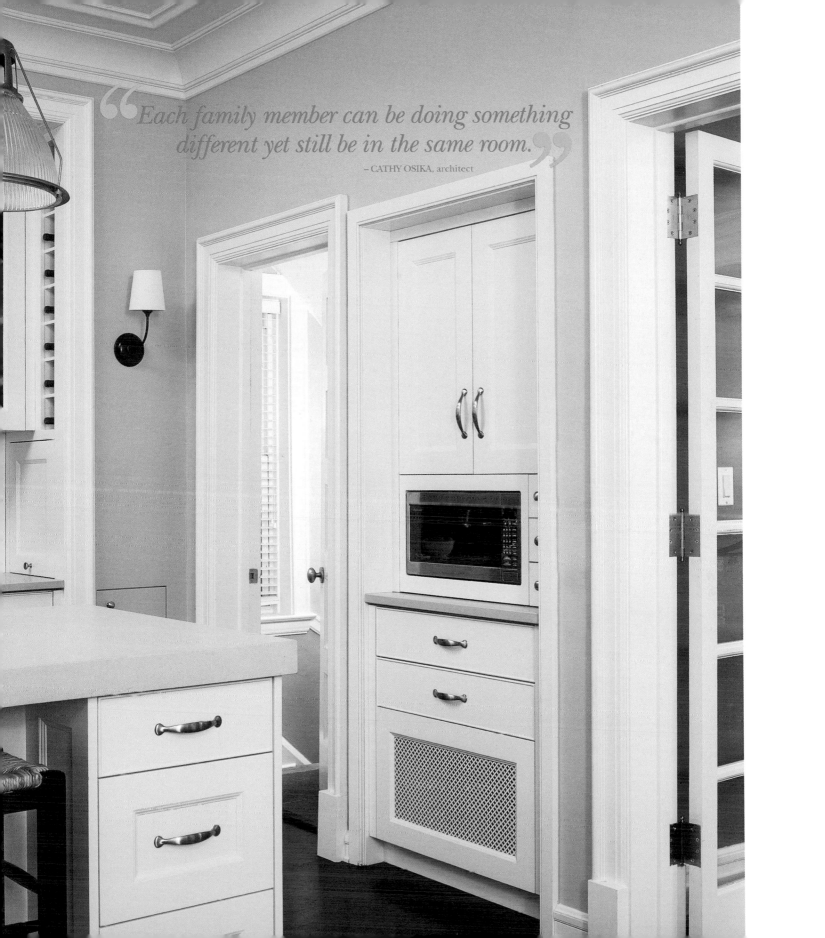

"Each family member can be doing something different yet still be in the same room."

– CATHY OSIKA, architect

Appliances plus

State-of-the-art commercial-style appliances ensure that a kitchen can handle the needs of a contemporary family. Their stainless-steel faces offer a timeless material that meshes with the historical leanings of the space. If you have young children, consider special stainless-steel finishes that don't show fingerprints. In this setting, the reflective surfaces work with the white cabinetry to make the kitchen cheerful for gathering.

The new kitchen connects to the dining room via French doors (above)—a feature that repeats throughout the house. The built-in banquette (left) boosts storage and seating for the room. Abutting the desk (opposite) with the banquette area keeps family members close and encourages communication.

ACCESSIBLE DESIGN

Planning for the future and the comfort of every family member in every stage of life was the focus of this Coronado, California, kitchen remodeling. Adaptive, unobtrusive features make the kitchen comfortable for a person in a wheelchair as well as for children and adults of every age.

"The kitchen was designed to be an age-in-place update for clients who are in their 50s," explains kitchen designer Richard Gatling. "Most of the house is on one level. For added accessibility, the aisles are either

Pendent lights (left) are one of four lighting sources in this kitchen. Attached to dimmer switches, the pendants offer both task and mood lighting. The wide aisle can accommodate a walker or wheelchair (opposite). Ample counterspace next to the refrigerator provides a place to transfer cooled items. The landing areas also provide workspace where you need it, saving time in food preparation.

This striking red service bar offers counterspace for informal "pull-up" dinners or for casual buffet service. The area also provides additional workspace for another cook.

42 or 48 inches wide. There is not a 60-inch wheelchair turnaround space inside the kitchen itself, but there is one adjacent. The way the kitchen is arranged, it is easy for two or three people to work in it comfortably even if one had a wheelchair or crutches."

To ensure accessibility for people of all ages and abilities, locate the main storage cabinets below counter height. Add glass inserts to upper cabinet doors to create display areas in the hard-to-reach places. Choose pull-style handles instead of knobs, because they can be gripped with the edge of the hand, a more comfortable position for those with arthritis. Add a handy walk-in pantry to provide easy-access storage for dry goods and serving pieces.

For cooking ease Gatling configured the kitchen with 48 inches of clear space in front of the range and provided ample landing space along one side for hot pots and pans. A steamer adjacent to the range reduces

CONTINUED ON PAGE 70

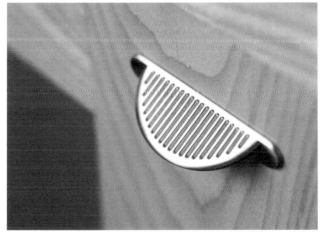

Front lever handles make it easy to control the range burners (left) from a seated position. Counterspace on each side of the range means some prep work can be completed at the stove and hot pots can be easily transferred off the flame. The owners requested a built-in steamer (top) so that they can cook healthy meals without having to carry heavy pans of water to the stove top. Pull handles like these (above) require less leverage and mobility than knobs.

Open Access

When planning your kitchen consider these adjustments to ensure that the room accommodates people of all ages and abilities.

Aisle space. Kitchen traffic lanes are typically about 3 feet wide, but the wider aisles in this kitchen make maneuvering wheelchairs and walkers easier. To allow for wheelchair turnaround, plan 5 feet of aisle space.

Accommodating appliances. For the easiest access choose wall ovens with side-hinge doors (and a separate cooktop with knee space below). The chef here opted for a professional-style range with two ovens because of its precision cooking capabilities and accessible front controls. To reduce the possibility of burns, the wheeling chef would use only the front burners. Position the microwave low enough so that it can be reached from a sitting position but high enough that it doesn't open into knees or armrests. Undercounter refrigerator and freezer drawers are equally accommodating to users of all abilities. Side-by-side refrigerators are another option; most of the storage drawers and bins are accessible to everyone regardless of their height. Plan for two sinks, one at standard 36-inch height for standing users and one 5 or 6 inches lower for sitters. Move water supply lines to the back of the sink to prevent hot pipes from burning bare legs.

Friendly finishes. Choose cabinetry with a distressed or natural-tone finish so that dings will not stand out—and may even add more character. Prefinished hardwood floors are firm and smooth under feet and wheels, making them a logical choice for any kitchen. Tile is another option, but grout joints need to be flush with the tile surface—otherwise every bump may be felt. Vinyl also works well but choose a high-quality variety that can withstand the wear of wheels. Choose a bullnose shape for counters to give arms a comfortable edge to rest on and to prevent denting and bruising that sharp, square edges can cause.

Accessible storage. Store everyday items such as dishes, pots, and pans in base cabinets equipped with roll-out shelves to cut down on reaching. Install wall cabinets that are 15 to 18 inches deep instead of the usual 12 inches. This increases the storage capacity of the shelves and makes the units jut out farther for easier access. Rather than equipping a walk-in or roll-in pantry closet with a swing-out door, choose a pocket door to allow a wheelchair to enter and exit easily.

Dishwasher drawers that flank the sink require less bending when loading and unloading.

the need for lugging pots filled with water that are required for typical stovetop boiling.

To make cleanup comfortable, two single-drawer top-mount dishwashers provide an easy reach for both the wheelchair-bound and those with aching backs who prefer to bend and stoop less. Multiple light sources—including skylights, undercabinet lights, recessed fixtures, and pendants—make it easier to see regardless of vision impairment. For more advice on kitchen lighting, see page 184.

To the right of the refrigerator and dining room entrance, a built-in cabinet with open shelves and a pair of drawers offers easy-access storage (left). A built-in beverage center (above), complete with a sink and icemaker, enables guests to help themselves to refreshments.

Numbers to Know

The National Kitchen & Bath Association recommends these guidelines when planning an accessible kitchen:

Comfortable reach. Locate door handles, appliances, and electrical outlets and switches 15 to 48 inches above the floor so that anyone can reach them comfortably.

Aisle and approach room. Aisles that are 4 feet wide comfortably accommodate wheelchairs and are recommended for multicook kitchens. Plan 5 feet of clear space for wheelchair turnarounds; ideally the kitchen should have two turnarounds, one near the refrigerator and one near the cooktop or sink.

Knee clearances and toe-kicks. Wheelchair users require knee clearances that are 27 inches high, 30 inches wide, and 19 inches deep. Similarly, extra-wide 9×6-inch toe-kicks allow wheelchair users to pull up closer to counters. Some cabinet manufacturers offer these deeper and wider toe-kicks as an option when you order; most other cabinets can be modified.

Faucets and hot water. Hands-free faucets that turn on with a sensor reduce the necessity to reach. Single-handle lever faucets are easier to turn on and off than two-handle varieties. To prevent scalding turn your hot water down to 120 degrees.

Doors and handles. Plan for a clear door opening of at least 36 inches. Equip entrance doors, cabinet doors, and drawers with lever or cup handles because they are easier to operate than knobs.

Windows. Casement windows are the easiest to operate from a sitting position. Install windows 24 to 30 inches above the floor so that wheelchair users can open, close, and easily see out of them.

A niche below the microwave stores small appliances right where they are used. Pullout baskets (above right) in the island make it easy to store and retrieve veggies and utensils. Wood plank floors allow smooth wheeling from one activity zone to the next.

DESIGN GALLERY
Comfort Zones

People get together in the kitchen more than any other area in the home. Bring living room comfort to this workplace with enticing art displays, cushy area rugs, and cozy gathering spaces.

1

2

1. In place of the usual pair of stools in front of a bar, allow room for bench seating and a dining table. Step up the style with art niches above the peninsula.

2. Bring the warmth of a fire into the kitchen by adding a double-sided fireplace.

3. A built-in seat turns a corner into a cozy dining spot.

4. Displays of art and collectibles take the utilitarian edge off the kitchen.

5. Make eating at the island feel as cozy as dining in a fine restaurant with a table-height extension and two comfortable dining chairs.

3

5

CHAPTER 2

Style Influences

It's easy to change your clothing to reflect a mood, but the style you choose
for your kitchen needs to be a comfortable fit for years to come.

The style you choose for your kitchen is as personal as your wardrobe, but the look of your kitchen is a choice you will live with for much longer than your clothing selections. If you're having difficulty determining what you can live with, consider this:

"The number one question to ask about the elements, colors, and patterns you are considering for your kitchen is, 'Would I wear this if it were a piece of clothing?'" says residential space planner and kitchen designer Richard Landon of Bellevue, Washington. "Whatever you wear sets a mood and obliquely communicates your feelings and ideas. How much more is your kitchen able to do the same thing, depending on how you dress it?"

To help you decide, turn the page and try on a few styles to see if one feels like a comfortable fit.

A curved range alcove lends the look of an old-fashioned hearth to this country French kitchen (opposite). High ceilings and a sleek hood bring modern style to an Arts and Crafts-style work core (left).

CLEAN COUNTRY

If you love the idea of a convivial country kitchen but you don't want the space to appear cluttered or cute, consider this elegant Southern rendition of farmhouse style. The space demonstrates that you can plan the storage you need without filling the upper walls with cabinetry—a look that can visually overwhelm a kitchen. To create this surprising fusion of clean contemporary and Low Country charm, kitchen designer Regina Garcia combined distressed-look black cabinetry, hardwood

Wide spacing between upper cabinets (opposite) helps emphasize the openness of the kitchen and minimizes the heft of the cabinetry. In the eating area (above), Louis XV-style chairs are fashioned from transparent acrylic.

flooring, vintage-style fittings and fixtures, and formal draperies—all in a sleek open space. Modern takes on classic forms play up the theme of past meeting present—a hutch with polka-dot glass doors and linen-shaded pendants above the island, for example. Most notable, a curved, mirrored niche behind the range echoes the shape of an old-fashioned hearth presented in a fresh context. Other reflective surfaces, such as the stainless-steel appliances and chrome fixtures, offset the dark cabinets. Brazilian granite, silk drapery fabric, and shades of green on the walls provide an elegant finish.

A matching distressed black panel disguises the dishwasher in the island (above) and allows the farmhouse sink and gooseneck faucet to become the friendly focal point. The pot filler (top right) introduces another vintage element with contemporary convenience. Cylindrical pendants (right) with linen shades supply artistic interest and practical lighting above the island.

The island makes the work core efficient, and the beaded board sides infuse the room with farmhouse flair. Silk draperies at the window lend elegance.

Reflective surfaces, such as the stainless-steel range, the mirrored inset above, and green glass tiles on the backsplash, help balance the use of black cabinetry.

Design Tip

Consider these elements to bring a clean country spirit to your kitchen:

• Start with distressed-finish cabinetry that's painted or stained but keep the spacing airy.

• Include plenty of reflective surfaces, such as stainless steel, chrome faucets, clear and patterned glass doors, glass tiles, and mirrored surfaces.

• Add the warmth of wood, such as flooring and some stained-wood countertops.

• Introduce a few classic designs fashioned from contemporary materials. Lighting and seating often combine the past and present.

The distressed black door offers a classic frame for the whimsical polka-dot glass panel (above left). A natural-tone countertop (left) provides visual relief for the predominantly dark piece. Old and new juxtapose with a state-of-the-art refrigerator (above) nestled into a bank of made-to-look-old cabinets.

TRUE-BLUE TRADITIONS

Pair a classic color combination, such as blue and white, with tried-and-true recessed-panel cabinetry and you've gained winning traditional style. In this kitchen, dark glaze gracefully ages the blue island base while a blue granite countertop offers a reminder that traditional style often nods to an era of elegance. Creamy white perimeter cabinets combine with two skylights and an abundance of chrome accents to give the room a luminous glow and an air of tranquillity.

CONTINUED ON PAGE 87

Pale blue walls inject an element of cool color (left) in a room dominated by white cabinetry and a white tile backsplash. Even the dinnerware (below) reinforces the mostly white scheme.

An apron-front sink (above) and a scalloped window treatment lend charm to the cleanup area. Rubbed edges give the white cabinetry (below) a weathered look.

Cove tiles give the island countertop (above) an elegant, traditional finished edge.

Design Tip

Invite traditional style home with these key features:

• Simple recessed-panel cabinets initiate this time-honored design.

• Weathered and distressed finishes promote a sense of history.

• Furniture styling, such as feet tucked into toe-kicks and turned legs on island ends, creates the illusion of fine, freestanding furnishings.

• Classic patterns—toile, stripes, or chintz, for example—lend color and interest.

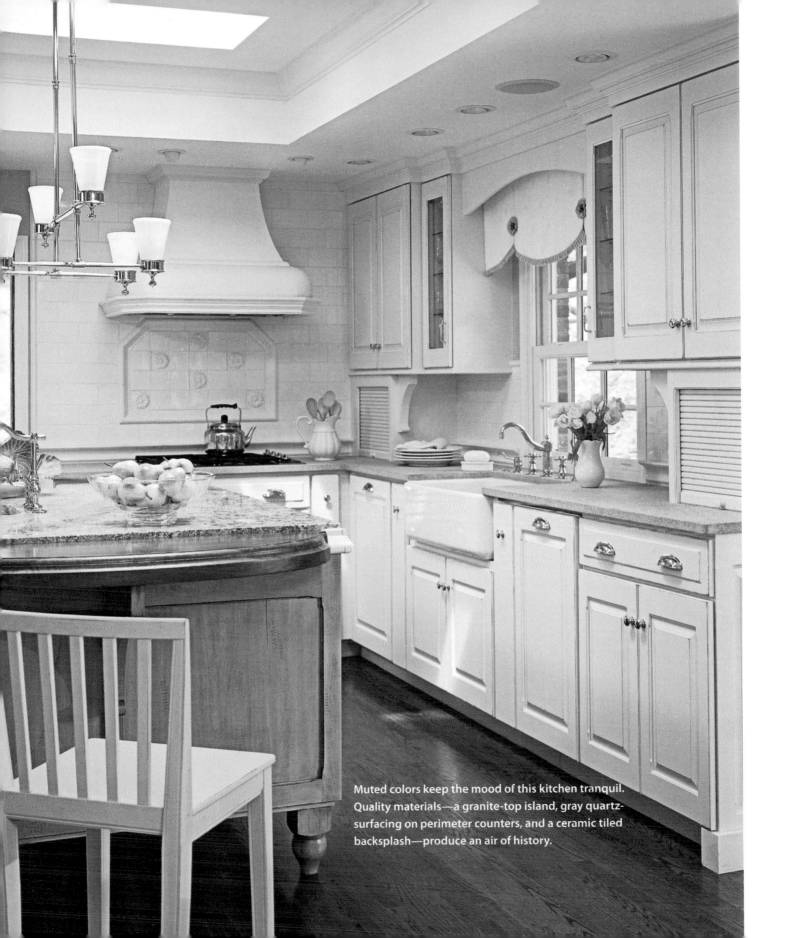

Muted colors keep the mood of this kitchen tranquil. Quality materials—a granite-top island, gray quartz-surfacing on perimeter counters, and a ceramic tiled backsplash—produce an air of history.

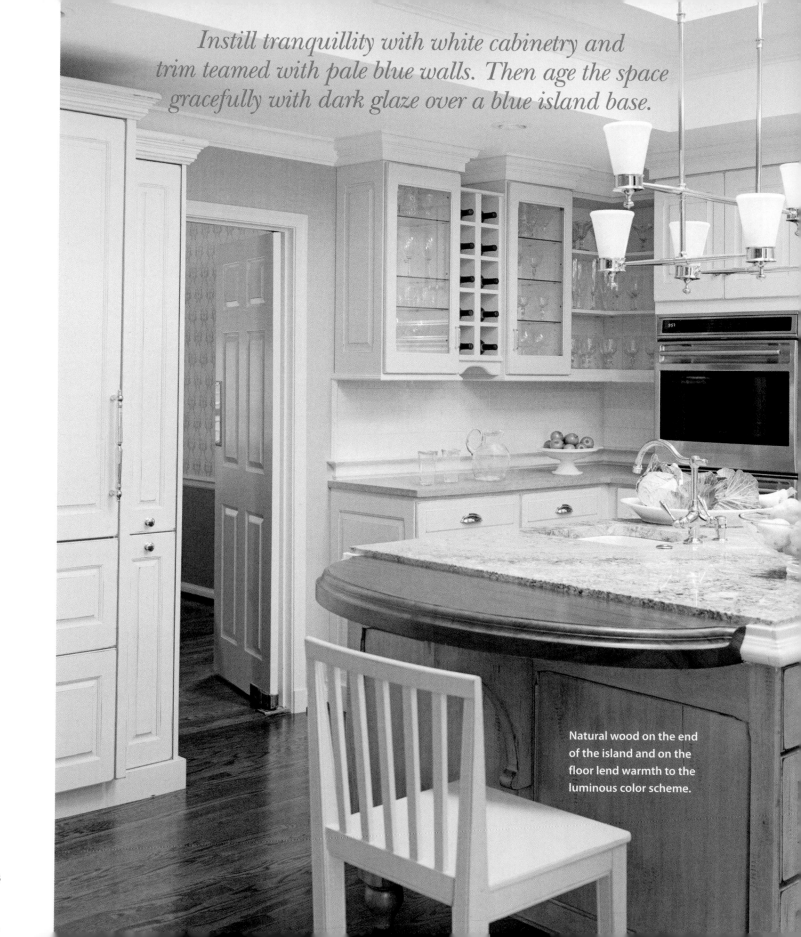

Instill tranquillity with white cabinetry and trim teamed with pale blue walls. Then age the space gracefully with dark glaze over a blue island base.

Natural wood on the end of the island and on the floor lend warmth to the luminous color scheme.

One of the secrets to maintaining an air of the past in a traditional kitchen is to keep modern components as unobtrusive as possible. Here matching white cabinet panels for the refrigerator and dishwasher work with the apron-front sink and vintage-style faucet to transport the room back in time.

When designing a kitchen with a monochromatic or pale color scheme, introduce interest with understated texture and tone-on-tone pattern. In this setting subtle textures, such as sanded edges on the cabinets and crackle-finish backsplash tiles, create a sense that the space has gained character as it aged. Gray quartz-surfacing countertops keep the look soft while providing a material that's practical and durable. For a flair of warmth, use wood flooring underfoot.

Heirloom stemware sparkles in glass-front cabinets (above left) flanking a wine rack. Outfitted with legs, the island (left) resembles furniture. The microwave oven (above) is tucked into one side of the island, keeping it handy without interrupting the old-fashioned feel of the room.

Sleek and dressy with its chocolate-olive cabinetry color, this contemporary kitchen is elegant and warm. Sheer drapery panels lend a soft, graceful touch to the dramatic arched window (opposite).

CALM CONTEMPORARY

With today's active lifestyles and hectic schedules, the uncluttered character of contemporary style offers relaxing rewards in the kitchen. If you're concerned that this straightforward look works only with new, streamlined houses, consider this 1914 Spanish Mediterranean home. In the kitchen owner and interior decorator Greg Mewbourne transformed the look from casual to modern simply by painting the maple wood cabinets and window trim a deep chocolate-olive hue. Almost-black and black simplify any kitchen's furnishings and cabinetry, yielding a sleek, elegant look. For this space, the deep color complements the existing polished French limestone floor and the almond-color Ghibili granite countertops. The new cabinet color grounds the kitchen and makes it richer.

CONTINUED ON PAGE 93

An abstract painting (above) creates a colorful kitchen focal point. Preserve artwork by hanging it away from the cooktop. An automotive paint shop transformed these metal stools (below) with white paint.

Design Tip

Bring in contemporary style with elements such as these:

• Flat door cabinets keep the look clean. Full-overlay doors minimize visual interruptions as well.

• Select simple cabinet hardware, such as round or oval knobs or sleek bars.

• Edit belongings to display minimal accessories for an uncluttered feel while providing color.

• Wood flooring and furnishings and sand-tone natural stone materials lend additional warmth.

The retro feel of the storage console (above) fits the modern styling of the kitchen. The golden hues of the wood also complement the polished French limestone flooring.

Add interest at the back of a countertop by displaying an unusual piece. This antique clock face fits perfectly at the back of the serving niche.

For a contemporary kitchen, painting cabinets a dark color conveys warmth and sophistication.

Contemporary style needn't be cold and uninviting. To warm up a kitchen, you can add stained wood floors and furnishings and introduce colorful accessories. Mewbourne, for example, brought in a wood serving console that offers the clean, glamorous lines of 1940s Hollywood style. A red cloisonné lamp and an abstract painting provide more color and inviting personality to the vignette.

There's room for other unexpected pairings with contemporary style, such as the antique clock face on display here and the floor-to-ceiling sheers used to soften the window and filter the light.

Reflective surfaces such as this stainless-steel range and the glass-door cabinet (left) offer visual relief amid dark cabinetry. The honed finish and simple edge treatment on the granite countertops (above left and above) complement the simplicity of contemporary style.

FRENCH BORN

Stepping into a country French-style kitchen is like traveling to another time and place. This cozy, relaxed look features a strong connection to the past, weathered woods, and cabinets that appear to be freestanding pieces of furniture.

"In an old French home, there would have been a hearth and a variety of freestanding storage pieces that the owners purchased over decades," kitchen designer Beth Merrell explains. "To achieve a time-honored look here, we mixed woods, finishes, and door styles to make the room appear as though it was furnished over time."

Reproduction faucets give the beverage center (above) vintage appeal.

Design Tip

Bring a cozy country French ambience to your kitchen by incorporating a few of these signature design elements:

• Choose Provençal fabrics such as toile de Jouy and Avignon stripes and florals.

• Look for antiques and reproduction furnishings with European origins.

• Combine weathered painted surfaces and distressed wood finishes.

• Outfit cabinetry with tarnished and distressed metal hardware.

• Use saturated colors such as deep reds, sunflower yellows, and cobalt blues.

The fine French look is old-fashioned, but the function is newfangled. Step-saving features include multiple dishwasher drawers (hidden behind cabinetry panels), two sinks, a professional range, and a restaurant-capacity refrigerator and freezer.

Hardworking, vintage-look natural surfaces are key. In this room countertops are Verdi granite and creamy limestone. Hickory reclaimed from a barn covers the floor. Rugged limestone tiles in a running bond pattern age the range wall. You'll also want to choose painted finishes that look centuries old. The remaining walls feature a buttery yellow glazed, stuccolike finish that appears to have darkened over time.

French-style accessories feature soft curves and intricate detailing. Shop flea markets and antiques stores for authentic French finds. In this space the finishing touches are native to France: pottery from Provence, a vintage stained-glass window from Avignon, and an antique pot rack and a chandelier from Paris.

Though the copper sink and faucets on the island (left) are new, they have the look of weathered antiques. Green granite counters enhance the effect. French dinnerware (above left) fills the displays. French copper pots (above) are both stylish and functional—the owners cook with them. Country French chairs with a worn paint finish (opposite) pull up to a metal-base table in the breakfast nook.

"*To achieve a time-honored look here, we mixed woods, finishes, and door styles to make the room appear as though it was furnished over time.*"

– BETH MERRELL, kitchen designer

Warm maple cabinets, orange basket liners, and pendent lights create a cozy ambience in this eclectic-style kitchen (above). Tubular-style steel shelves in front of the sink window match the stainless-steel appliances and fixtures and provide extra display space.

ECLECTIC ENERGY

If you have an appreciation for all things beautiful, an eclectic kitchen may be the style choice for you. Mixing and matching is the mantra in kitchens like this one; style elements come from different periods and places.

The key to pulling a collection of attractive yet unrelated pieces together is to find or create some commonality in each element. In this kitchen unity

Fabric-lined baskets (above left) keep the atmosphere casual and island storage neat. A large tambour-door appliance garage (left) ensures the countertops remain clutter-free and encourages a sleek, modern appearance. A glass door embedded with reeds (above) opens to reveal pullout spice racks. (This cabinet is to the left of the appliance garage.)

is achieved by way of a relaxed attitude. The cabinets and fixtures feature a smooth, contemporary, and unpretentious facade. Accessories and storage baskets have a vintage European feel, yet their laid-back, easy appearance makes them look right at home.

Surfaces connect to nature and include maple cabinets, soapstone perimeter counters, travertine floors, and a rain-forest marbletop center island with a raised walnut cutting board.

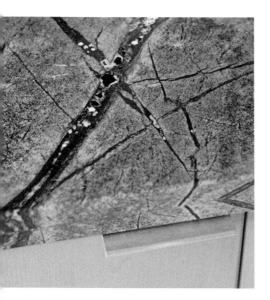

Marble mined in Africa (left) tops a portion of the island and one counter and defines the kitchen's color scheme. Translucent door panels (right), some embedded with bamboo reeds, combine with handpainted ceramics and a carved wooden vase to bring a touch of the Orient to the eating area. Dollops of orange unite this portion of the kitchen with the rest of the space.

Design Tip

Ensure your eclectic kitchen looks pulled together by following these design tips:

Make a color connection. In this kitchen the colors in the marble define the color scheme and create a visual tie between the honey tones of the cabinets and the sage green walls. You can create additional color connections through the use of color-matched knobs, table linens, rugs, upholstery, and pottery.

Choose formal or casual pieces. This kitchen features a straightforward, comfortable look including flat-front cabinet doors and unpretentious storage baskets. If you prefer a more formal attitude, choose items with more intricate details, such as raised-panel cabinet doors and handcarved corbels.

COTTAGE WARMTH

Cottage style melds elements that are both humble and high-class, yielding a look that is warm and romantic. To bring this comfortable style home, consider this kitchen, which welcomes you in with its deliberate imperfections and delightful burst of color.

Cabinets that mimic old-fashioned freestanding furnishings provide a solid anchor for setting a casual pace in any kitchen. A merging of ivory-painted and honey-stained pine cabinets—artfully capped off with a vivid green hutchlike display shelf on one wall—creates

Turned legs give this island the character of a farmhouse kitchen table. Cream-color walls set off the wood beam architecture. Ladderback chairs with rush seats (opposite) speak to the vintage roots of this style.

Cabinetry in a cottage kitchen shouldn't appear pristine. In this kitchen the pine cabinets feature white glaze that collects in the impressions—appearing as though an old coat of paint has worn off. Cream-color paint on the remaining cabinets is distressed and sanded for a weathered guise.

the illusion that this work area and gathering space evolved over many years.

Other surfaces and components are chosen to promote the appearance of age and variety, giving the kitchen a well-worn cottage feel. The mottled golden finish on the floor tiles is rustic and hides dirt. Adding fabric softens hard edges and brings in cottage color and pattern. In this kitchen plaid and floral fabrics have vintage flair and provide an unassuming contrast to the almost-regal arched alcove above the stove. Completing the theme are venerable limestone farmhouse-style sinks with faucets of darkened metal—a material that reappears on some of the cabinets.

Homey fabrics, such as ginghams and ticking, are integral to cottage style, but they can be functional too. The floral beneath the window (left) hides small appliances, while the plaid (above) keeps the television under wraps in the island. Collectible milk glass serving pieces (above left) reinforce the cottage look.

Design Tip

Use some of the following elements to create cottage style:

• Include vintage floral patterns in fabrics, dishware, or wallcoverings.

• Display garden items, such as a wooden bench or ironwork from a gate, as unexpected artwork.

• Mix vintage and antique furnishings of various origins.

• Bring in white-painted wood, muted colors associated with the beach, or fresh colors that make a garden connection.

• Incorporate beaded board and tongue-and-groove panels.

Lively green color, scalloped edges, and tongue-and-groove backing give this hutchlike display shelf (opposite and left) cottage appeal. Hidden behind pine panels and flanking the sink are a dishwasher and a pullout trash bin. White paneled doors blend the refrigerator (above) with the wall cabinetry.

CRAFTSMAN STYLE

Form and function unite in a kitchen that draws inspiration from the Arts and Crafts movement of the late 19th and early 20th centuries. Favoring the handmade over the mass-produced, this British movement became known in America as Craftsman style. Furniture and architecture from this period featured simple geometric designs, natural surfaces, and warm earthy colors.

Architects James Blair and Ian Lawrence envisioned a Craftsman connection for this kitchen. Four squares grouped in a larger square—a common graphic element in Craftsman kitchens—serve as the room's primary design motif. New Douglas fir cabinets sporting the four-square design complement an existing beamed ceiling. The ceiling itself

This stylish yet low-maintenance kitchen underscores the Craftsman-era mantra: Meld form with function. Natural surfaces and handcrafted rectilinear designs permeate the room (opposite). Craftsman-style pendent lights (left) illuminate the serving counter.

gained large skylights and halogen track fixtures to help brighten the windowless space. Additional windowlike cutouts high on the sink wall borrow light from the adjacent skylight-lit hallway. Behind the sink, a mirrored backsplash—a departure from the typical elements of the style—reflects additional light and accentuates the reflective quality of the stainless-steel appliances and fixtures. Slate tile floors complement the naturalist design. Concrete counters were stained onsite and wear the same earth-tone tints as the floor.

"The contemporary Craftsman motif is warm, friendly, and casual," says Blair. "The style's cozy, comfortable ambience makes it a natural draw for friends and family."

All the surfaces—Douglas fir cabinets, concrete countertops, and natural slate floors (left)—were chosen for their low-maintenance properties and naturally good looks. A mirrored backsplash behind the sink (opposite) creates a sense of spaciousness.

Rippled glass in the cabinet doors (opposite above left) adds texture. The concrete counters (opposite above right) were stained to match the slate backsplash and floors. The stainless-steel faucet (opposite left) is clean and contemporary. Time-honored shapes, such as the recessed cabinetry panels (opposite), reflect Craftsman style. Slate tiles on the floor and the breakfast bar (right) contain all the colors of the kitchen.

> *The style's cozy, comfortable ambience makes it a natural draw for friends and family.*
> —JAMES BLAIR, architect

DESIGN GALLERY
Color Inspiration

No matter what style you choose for your kitchen, you'll need a color palette. Explore your home and surroundings and you'll find things as ordinary as these can nurture the creative process.

1

2

1. Bring the outdoors inside with a color scheme inspired by a garden or bouquet.

2. Use fabric or rugs to connect your color selections or let these textiles (or even a favorite piece of clothing) launch a new look.

3. Translate the colors in a piece of artwork to your kitchen environment. If they work in a painting, they'll work in the room.

4. Tiles can influence palette and motifs.

5. Let what you love— including china—provide design inspiration.

3

4

5

A small bumpout (opposite) can expand the kitchen's usefulness to include gathering spaces (this page).

CHAPTER 3

Plan the Project

*Explore possible paths to your dream kitchen—a facelift, a footprint
renovation, a bumpout, or a full room addition could meet your goals.*

To transform your kitchen desires into reality, assess your family's needs. A simple facelift is the most cost-effective solution. In these updates simple changes, such as refacing cabinetry, adding new hardware, and replacing a surface or two, give a kitchen a new look.

If your kitchen needs more than a fresh face, consider a complete renovation within the existing walls. The space is gutted and remodeled anew. Appliances may change locations and windows may be added, but the walls remain in the original locations.

If you want a larger kitchen, combine existing rooms to gain space. Otherwise an addition might be the only way to gain the space you need. When considering an addition check with local building officials to learn setback restrictions and easements. Knowing these will help you determine how and where you can build on your property. Even a simple bumpout can require a zoning variance.

FACELIFT REFRESHER

When you want to transform the look of a kitchen but retain existing cabinetry, you've opted for a remodeling strategy known as a facelift. In this scenario surfaces and components are renewed or exchanged, allowing you to complete the redo quickly because little, if any, demolition is necessary. Alternatively if you're not in a hurry, a kitchen facelift allows you to pay as you go. "A facelift lends itself to working in stages," says Anna Marie DeMayo, the designer of this Kansas City-area kitchen. "Spend your remodeling funds on countertops one month, paint another month, and so on."

You will also find that a facelift will cost less because you don't have to buy new cabinetry. This kitchen, for example, retained the original countertops, flooring, and cabinet boxes but traded the modern flat-front doors for traditional paneled ones. While lower cabinets and the island base remained black, new white paint provided a lighter look for upper cabinets. Glass panels in some doors introduce charm and display space. "If you think you want to refresh existing cabinets," DeMayo

Paint, new cabinet doors and hardware, crisp white subway tiles for the backsplash, and a few other simple changes transformed this kitchen from '80s mod (above) to country French refreshing (right).

New window treatments (above) punctuate the kitchen with more country French flavor and cheerful color.

before

says, "make sure they feel solid and that drawers operate smoothly. Otherwise, they aren't worth keeping."

Hardware. "Changing the cabinet knobs or pulls is one of the quickest and least expensive ways to change the look of a kitchen," DeMayo says. "If your kitchen has 1980s antique brass pulls, then go for chrome or brushed nickel and you've instantly updated the space."

Countertops. If you don't like your existing countertops, you can exchange them for an upgrade material. Or, as a temporary fix for laminate or wood, paint the countertop. (Look for a paint recommended for use on laminate.)

Sink and faucet. Whether you keep your countertops or replace them, a new sink and faucet can improve function and refresh the appearance. When keeping the old countertop, be sure to select a sink that fits the cutout in the countertop or plan to enlarge the opening. (Be sure the cabinet below is wide enough to hold a larger sink.)

Appliances. Some existing appliances can gain new style. The refrigerator in this kitchen received panels that match the new cabinet doors.

Lighting. Update lighting to bring your kitchen in line with the new look you have in mind. Exchanging

When a kitchen adjoins other rooms, continue the makeover materials for continuity. Paint and fabric provide the visual link.

121

new fixtures for old is a quick and fairly low-cost project.

Flooring. Often all the flooring needs is refreshing. Call in the steam cleaners to clean tile and grout, or have a wood floor professionally refinished. For temporary measures consider painting laminate, vinyl, or wood flooring. (Use quality primer and paint formulated for the material.)

Ceiling. Believe it or not, an outdated ceiling can drag down the look of your kitchen. "Always remove the 'popcorn' on a ceiling," DeMayo says. "It's time consuming, but a smooth finish is so much more attractive and up-to-date."

Fabric. New window treatments and seat covers can inject fresh color and pattern into your space for minimal investment.

A black iron chandelier (opposite above) provides a finishing touch for the facelift. The black finish on lower cabinets (opposite below left) is original (as is the countertop), but new hardware enhances the vintage theme. New sinks offer special features such as this cutting board accessory (opposite below right). The replacement faucet includes a pullout sprayer. Divided-light glass panels (above left) in some of the new upper doors provide display space. This charming pine fireplace facade (left) hides a black granite slab.

WITHIN THE FOOTPRINT

If you can't fit everything you need into your existing space, consider tearing out an interior wall to open your kitchen to another room, such as the dining room or family room. Incorporating adjacent spaces, such as closets, a mudroom, a hallway, a spare bedroom, or a pantry, may also provide the additional square footage you need.

In this home, kitchen designer Mick De Giulio reworked a separate kitchen and family room into one large, gracious gathering space.

If you're planning a large kitchen like this one, consider two center islands instead of one long one—two islands can save steps when moving from one activity center to another. The large island topped with granite and a smaller island topped with brown fossil stone are centered to facilitate traffic flow throughout the room. In the renovated great-room (opposite), fireside seating and a nearby dining table enable guests to be near the cooks.

To make a new grand space feel intimate and inviting, De Giulio suggests varying ceiling heights and surface coverings to help delineate the various activity centers. In this great-room De Giulio had a beamed ceiling lowered over the kitchen's work area, which includes two islands, a beverage center, and a cleanup zone. The vaulted ceiling resumes at the far end of the great-room, where plush seating gathers around a new fireplace and overmantel equipped with a flat-panel television.

Black and white marble tile runs the length of the great-room (opposite). A thick area rug sets off the seating area. Although made from different stones, the two sinks (above left) feel cohesive due to identical faucets and parallel placement. White-painted cabinets and an enlarged window make the main cleanup center (left) feel cheerful and inviting.

For more visual separation De Giulio had the refrigerator wrapped in mesquite, the center island made out of cherry, and the beverage center made from walnut. White-painted cabinets bring contrast to the cleanup area. A similarly inspiring selection of surfacing materials includes scoon—a refined French limestone—around the range, Carrara marble around the sink, and a classic grid of black and white marble tile on the floor.

When reworking a room, always take stock of the existing window and door placement, De Giulio says. If the budget allows, consider enlarging and repositioning the panes to better frame views and bring in more light. In this space, the sink window was replaced with a bumpout, and larger windows were added to two walls in the sitting area.

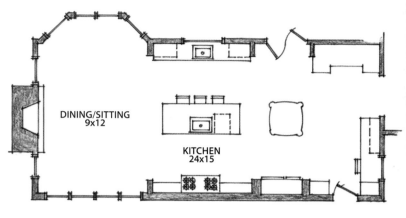

SAME FOOTPRINT
Removing a wall between the kitchen and family room forms one gathering space for cooking, dining, and relaxing.

The walnut beverage center (left) hides countertop appliances behind a mirrored panel backsplash. A variety of surface selections and finishes helps make the large space (opposite) feel more intimate and creates a feeling that the room was furnished over time.

Tame Open Spaces

Controlling the traffic flow and corralling activities into different sections of one large room help maintain a functional and appealing ambience. A center island separates passersby from the cook's workstation. Columns, steps, and changing ceiling heights can also create visual boundaries between rooms without closing off pathways. Partial walls may also be used to separate two rooms without closing them off completely, and the walls may double as built-in storage space, countertop workspace, or a serving area.

SIMPLE BUMPOUT

Loosely defined, a bumpout is any addition in which an exterior wall has been moved out several feet to make a room larger. Cantilevered bumpouts involve pushing out an exterior wall no more than 3 or 4 feet—the distance that wooden floor joists can be cantilevered without adding foundation supports. Cantilevered bumpouts are typically the least expensive solutions because they don't require any changes to the existing foundation. The largest bumpouts can span the length of an exterior wall, adding space to one or more rooms.

The range (below) provides the cooking precision the owners longed for. Locating the fridge on the wall (right) creates a compact work triangle, which saves steps when moving from one workspace to the next.

A 12×3-foot bumpout made this kitchen, designed by architect Mike Kastner, into the heart of the home. Note that even a 3-foot-wide bumpout may require additional foundation support to allow crawlspace for new plumbing lines, as was necessary for the sink wall in this kitchen. Changing the foundation pushes up the price by several thousand dollars, Kastner says, but doing so is often necessary to make a kitchen layout as hardworking as possible.

Setback restrictions can also limit the size and placement of a bumpout. The owners of this home had to apply for a variance to receive permission to build within 2 feet of their property line.

The 3 extra feet of width provide enough space for the refrigerator to move to an adjacent wall. This made the workspace more efficient and allowed room for banquette seating on the wall where the fridge once stood (see page 134).

Reusing the bricks that were removed from the original exterior wall makes this new bumpout (left) look as if it has always been a part of the home. Matching shingles, roof pitch, and eaves ensure a seamless appearance. The change in ceiling heights (above) delineates where the existing kitchen ended and the new space begins. A display shelf (right) provides a spot for showing off collectibles.

New cherry cabinets, white woodwork, and oak floors complement the finishes found elsewhere in the 1930s-era home.

To make the new 12×11-foot space seem even larger, Kastner added a wall of windows and extended the panes as close to the apex of the addition as possible. "Adding the windows sacrificed a few cabinets, but the sunlight and views made it an excellent trade," he says. "To create as much storage as possible, we extended the cabinets to the ceiling line on the adjacent walls and added glass-sided cabinets to both sides of the banquette."

Professional-grade appliances and a small yet functional center island maximize the kitchen's efficiency and make it comfortable for cooking and entertaining. "The island directs traffic out of the way of the cooks and provides a great place to serve appetizers and set serving bowls during dinner," Kastner says. "It illustrates what 3 extra feet of width can buy."

Hinged tops on the banquette seats (above) provide access to storage. Cabinets with glass doors (opposite) open on three sides, making it easy to access dishes and glassware. The new banquette provides intimate seating.

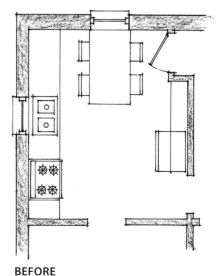

BEFORE

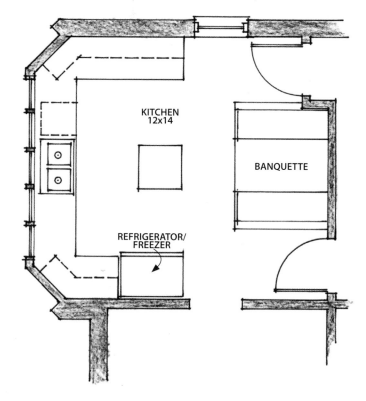

AFTER—SMALL BUMPOUT
Extending this kitchen 3 feet creates enough space to move the eating area outside the work core and allows room for a small center island.

WHOLE ROOM ADDITION

Adding on a full-size kitchen costs more than bumping out. But you might opt for this solution if:
• It's the only way to gain the gathering space and efficiency you need and desire.
• An addition would greatly improve traffic flow.
• Adding on lets you include more or larger windows and doors to improve views and outdoor access.

Residential designer Debra Toney and architect Mark Adcock cite similar motives for designing a kitchen addition for their Denver home. "This is a 1940s Tudor," Toney says, "and kitchens from that era are small and not for entertaining."

Square footage and function. The two-story addition offers a master suite upstairs and the kitchen downstairs. Because they were able to choose the square footage for the kitchen, the couple planned an extra-large island and generous 5-foot-wide aisles. "We wanted the wide aisles so that multiple cooks would be comfortable,"

The old kitchen space didn't go to waste—the designers outfitted it as a butler's pantry (above) that serves as a staging area between a formal dining room and the kitchen. Built-in bookshelves (left) run the length of a kitchen wall, framing the doorway to a potting room. Warm wood floors and Carrara marble countertops (opposite) provide classic visual links so this contemporary kitchen addition melds with the 1940s house.

Moldings, high ceilings, and classic stainless steel in this kitchen help smooth the transition between old and new. Sleek chrome hardware and the clean edge on the countertop (opposite above) speak to the modern-day heritage of the addition. An apron front on the sink and recessed panels in the cabinet doors (opposite below) recall vintage 1940s style.

Toney explains. "And the island is huge—the equivalent of two queen-size beds laid end to end—providing prep area for several helpers."

Traffic flow. The addition also improved the connection between the kitchen and the now-adjoining family room. With these spaces open to one another, parties, family activities, and conversation flow uninhibited. The island serves as traffic cop, corralling helpers in the work core and keeping guests and kids in the breakfast area and family room.

Improved views and accessibility. Because most additions offer three new exterior walls, window and door configurations can be designed to maximize the connection between indoors and out. Exterior openings in this addition improve the visual and functional connections to the outdoor dining and living areas.

Smooth transitions. Matching design details create coherence between new and existing spaces. "It is always important to look at the original architecture and pick up those design themes and elements to reuse for good visual continuity," Toney says. "Zero in on what is really special about the house, such as windows, cove ceilings, flooring, siding, and roof pitch."

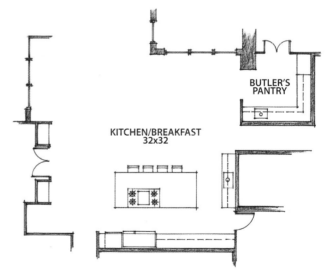

BUTLER'S PANTRY

KITCHEN/BREAKFAST 32x32

ROOM ADDITION
The addition positions the kitchen and breakfast area between the butler's pantry and the family room.

DESIGN GALLERY
Winsome Windows

Increase the size of your glass openings and add as many new windows as possible. The additional panes brighten and visually expand your kitchen and can also become art themselves.

1. An oval window heightens the charm of this classic cottage kitchen.

2. A window wraps a corner in this kitchen, allowing the scenery to take center stage.

3. Cabinets with glass panels front and back define spaces without confining them.

4. Transoms stack above these casement windows to extend drama and views to the ceiling.

5. Etched glass in these pocket doors reinforces the Victorian style of trimwork and cabinetry and allows light to filter from room to room.

CHAPTER 4

Cabinetry and Storage

Customize your storage to match

your individual requirements.

According to Chicago-based kitchen designer Mick De Giulio, "one-size-fits-all kitchens are a thing of the past." Today's homeowners are requesting kitchens that match their individual lifestyles as well as the style of their home. In many areas of the country that means designers are planning spaces that are more open and less filled with cabinets.

Walls of windows are becoming more common in kitchen design. This minimalist movement has a certain irony, says certified master kitchen and bath designer Kathleen Donohue of Eugene, Oregon. "Even though there are fewer cabinets in kitchens, we have more stuff to store than ever before. What that means is that homeowners should focus on 'walls of storage' rather than walls of cabinets—more walk-in pantries and blocks of cabinets—so there's still an appearance of open space."

Frosted glass doors (opposite) add visual interest to traditional paneled cabinetry. Well-planned storage allows every family member to reach what they need (left).

Pullout drawers organize pots and pans below the cooktop (right). The pop-up shelf (below) provides extra workspace for a blender and requires only a few extra seconds to pop in place. With an outlet installed inside the cabinet, the blender is always ready to go.

Lazy Susans (left) maximize storage in corner cabinets. A pullout spice rack (opposite above) makes more efficient use of cabinet storage. This custom drawer-style knife block (opposite below) keeps blades sharp.

FUNCTION FIRST

Instead of honing in on door styles and finishes, first think about how you want to use the space. "Think about which doors you open and close every day, which doors your kids will use most often, and you start thinking about the most efficient use of space," Kathleen Donohue explains.

When it comes to choosing storage systems, efficiency is the top priority. Certain swing-outs and pullouts may look great, but, Mick De Giulio cautions, they may cause you extra steps. "The least amount of motion required is key," he says. "Drawers are ideal. One motion, and you have what you need."

Easy care

Alan Hilsabeck Jr., a kitchen designer in Dallas, also suggests that cabinet buyers consider maintenance as much as style and storage capability. "Even here in Dallas, where we're very traditional by nature, we're seeing clients steer clear of heavy applied moldings—all those curlicues and carved spaces are difficult to dust and keep clean. Clients are opting for cleaner lines instead."

Material matters

Quality is also important. Solid hardwood doors are generally better than those made of fiberboard. Most cabinet doors are ¾ inch thick, but 1¼-inch doors look and feel much more substantial.

A cabinet's plywood sides and back should be ½ to ¾ inch thick, and shelves should be supported by steel pins instead of plastic clips.

Drawer bodies should be made of plywood, oak, or maple and ⅝ inch thick. Dovetail or good-quality mortise-and-tenon joints last longer than those that are nailed and glued. Wooden corner blocks also signify sturdy construction.

Cabinet finishes

Woods. Most cabinets are covered in a combination of solid-wood pieces and wood veneers. Solid-wood

cabinets are higher priced and feature a wider variety of grain patterns than wood veneers. All woods can be stained to achieve different looks. The range of appearance will vary greatly in some species, and different pieces of the same wood will take stain differently, so look at a variety of cabinetry samples before making your final selection. If the wood you like best is out of your price range, ask your cabinet dealer about compromises. Maple stained to resemble cherry will give you a look close to actual cherry, but it won't cost as much.(For cabinetry pricing information, see page 151).

Laminates. High-pressure laminates are made from durable and stain-resistant plastic resins that are available in a wide range of colors. Low-pressure laminates, often found on inexpensive shelves and closet organizers, may chip.

Vinyl films. Also known as thermofoil films, these are heat-laminated to a medium-density fiberboard (MDF) backing. Although vinyl film resembles a painted wood finish, the material is impervious to water and can be wiped down with a damp cloth.

Metals. For easy-to-clean surfaces and a contemporary setting, consider European frameless steel cabinets. Some are durable enough for outdoor use.

Stock, semicustom, or custom?

As manufacturing quality continues to increase, the lines between the three cabinetry types continue to blur. Stock cabinetry is typically less expensive than semicustom or custom because it is mass-produced. Though stock cabinetry features fewer size, style, and design options than semicustom or custom cabinets, the number of special features continues to increase, enabling buyers

The pullout spice drawer (above right) makes it easy to find what you need. Vertical dividers organize trays and cookie sheets in this narrow yet efficient space (center right). The appliance garage (right) keeps small appliances out of sight yet plugged in and ready to use.

These ultraefficient glides, installed below the cooktop, make it easy to grab the pan you need.

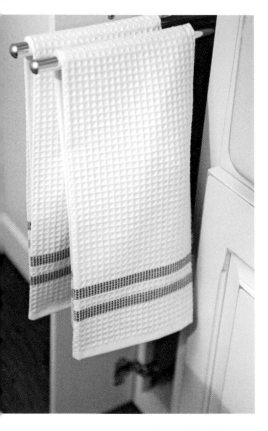

Located near the sink, these pullout rods (above) keep dish towels handy yet hidden. With customized storage drawers, cubbies, and hooks (right), this kitchen is organized to save time and steps.

to purchase many of the storage conveniences, such as appliance garages, recycling bins, and spice drawers, that were once reserved for custom cabinets. Because it is preassembled, stock cabinetry can often be delivered within a week or two of purchase.

Semicustom cabinets are similar to stock cabinets but offer a wider range of sizes, styles, and finishes. These cabinets are typically priced higher than stock cabinets and take longer for delivery—usually four to six weeks. As a cost-saving measure, large cabinet companies often offer semicustom cabinets to match stock units, allowing you to mix and match pieces to fit your dimensions and your budget.

Custom cabinets are made to order. The cabinetry fits your space and your tastes and is generally made of higher quality materials than stock or semicustom cabinetry. Because nothing is premade or warehoused, custom cabinets may require 10 to 12 weeks for delivery.

Composition

Whatever material or finish you select, choosing cabinetry to complement the architecture and other design elements of your kitchen—appliances, countertops, backsplashes, and flooring—requires the ability to see the overall picture. "I take a door with me to the manufacturer or the warehouse and I match it to everything else, from the faucets to the flooring," Hilsabeck says. He also takes it into the kitchen to see how light and wall color affect the look of the finish.

A restaurant-style rail installed on the backsplash (above) shows off copper pots and puts them within easy reach.

Skew the View

Using different types of glass can help you tune the look of cabinetry displays to achieve the effect you want.

  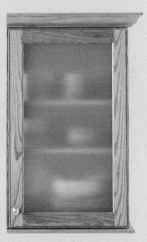

White everyday china (above left) becomes almost sculptural when viewed through ribbed glass, which accentuates the shapes and shadows and adds texture. Fine patterns show best when they can be viewed without interference as shown in this clear glass-front cabinet (above center). To tone down the appearance of brightly colored pieces, consider frosted glass (above right).

Shiny white laminate cabinets (above) lend a contemporary look to this seaside condo. Wide drawers make efficient use of space. Customize your cabinet interiors with dividers designed to hold specific items. In this cabinet (above right), horizontal shelves combine with vertical dividers to organize cookie sheets and large stock pots. The narrow island cabinet (right) puts empty space to work to organize spices and bottles.

Cabinetry Budget

Kitchen cabinetry, on average, accounts for about 60 percent of the budget for a kitchen renovation. Although that is a significant amount, certified master kitchen and bath designer Kathleen Donohue of Eugene, Oregon, says, "Fear not. Kitchen design is not just about the cabinets anymore. Today's kitchen design is much more holistic."

Cabinetry is more functional than ever. Responding to consumer demand for help with storage and organizing, cabinet manufacturers have introduced a wide range of features that make the most of available space inside cabinets and drawers. From stacked dividers for cutlery to tiered shelf storage and swing-out cabinet shelves, options allow you to turn cabinetry into a comprehensive, efficient storage system.

Here's what you can expect to pay for new kitchen cabinetry per linear foot, wall and base included:

BUDGET	BETTER	SPLURGE
$60–$200 • Stock/ready-to-assemble particleboard; finish choices: oak, maple, birch, white paint; three-quarter drawer extension hardware with 75-pound rating.	$150–$1,000 • Semicustom in more woods and finishes; dovetailed hardwood drawers with full-extension, 100-pound-rated hardware; plywood construction.	$600–$1,200+ • High-grade custom cabinetry; any size, shape, or finish; exotic woods.

A kitchen appears more spacious when open shelves alternate with cabinets (above left). A fitted silverware drawer (above) keeps utensils organized and can be removed for easy cleaning.

DESIGN GALLERY
Spirited Storage

A little bit of space can go a long way when you are storing bottles of wine, liqueurs, and other spirits. Uncork one of these clever storage solutions for your kitchen and let the party begin.

1. Hinged at the top, these doors with decorative glass inserts flip up to reveal a fully stocked bar.

2. Stacking bottles on an open bookcase shelf is a simple storage solution.

3. Custom shelves showcase a wine collection. A wooden lip on each shelf prevents the bottles from rolling off.

4. Combined with an arched display niche, this wine storage center serves as an attractive focal point.

5. A rarely used desk becomes a wine storage center with the addition of a bar sink and metal wine racks.

CHAPTER 5

Surface Solutions

Make your kitchen as beautiful and functional as possible
by choosing surfaces that match your tastes and your lifestyle.

Material choices for flooring, countertops, and backsplashes affect the look, the function, and the cost of your kitchen renovation. Your top priority when choosing these components should be how the materials function given how you, your family, and guests will use the space.

Your best dollar payback comes from equipping your kitchen with materials, fixtures, and features that have become the standard in comparably priced homes.

If you're planning to live in your house for years and resale is less of an issue, make material choices that are as personal as you please.

Bamboo flooring combines with stone counters and tile backsplashes (opposite) to provide textural contrast and easy care. Concrete counters (left) can be honed or polished and stained to match any decor.

The graining of soapstone (below) varies depending on where the rock was quarried. This flecked variety is mined in Vermont. The classic elegance of Carrara marble (right) pairs well with a matching mosaic marble backsplash.

Rare colors and unusual patterns of granite cost significantly more than more commonly occurring grays and beiges. This pricey granite counter (left) is quarried in northern regions and is flecked with vivid blue labradorite—a semiprecious stone.

Eucalyptus granite (above) is quarried in Brazil and is known for its unusual pattern. Slate tiles draw from a deep palette of green and black and add texture, pattern, and color to the floor of this creamy white kitchen (below right).

STONE

Stone is the heavyweight of surfacing. It can take a beating and is always in style. Stone slabs are heavier and more expensive than tiles but eliminate grout cleanup.

Granite
Granite is the most durable natural stone. It is virtually maintenance-free and impervious to stains, hot pots, and moisture.

Soapstone
This natural material starts out as a light gray color and then mellows to a dark warm charcoal after oiling and aging. Like granite it can withstand heat and moisture and, when regularly oiled, resists stains.

Slate
This multitone rough-hewn material is slightly more porous than granite but is nearly as durable. It can be sealed to prevent staining.

Marble and limestone
These timeless classics are porous stones, so they must be sealed regularly to reduce staining.

Design Tip

Whatever stone you choose, remember that glossy finishes have a tendency to show finger- and footprints and can be slippery when wet. For better traction choose a honed (textured) finish.

STONE LOOK-ALIKES

Quartz

This composite material brings nature and technology together in a stone look-alike that offers multiple color options. The material is made from crushed quartz mixed with an acrylic resin and resembles granite but with a little extra sparkle. Although extremely durable, it can be scorched by hot pots.

Solid-surfacing

Solid-surfacing requires little maintenance and is more resistant to scratches than laminate and more resistant to stains than marble. Cast entirely from acrylic resin, these surfaces are lighter in weight than stone and can be fabricated using regular woodworking tools. Sharp knives and hot pots can damage solid-surfacing, but because this faux stone is solid—the color runs throughout—sanding or buffing the surface can repair shallow scratches and burns. Inlays of contrasting colors can be used to create special effects. Once the countertop is installed, seams are undetectable, making cleanup easy. The ability to integrate a matching sink into the countertop is the material's greatest attraction.

Ceramic tiles

Clay-base ceramic tiles are extremely durable, easy to care for, and water-, stain-, heat- and wear-resistant. It is often difficult to tell ceramic impostors from natural stone. Tiles with a high-gloss finish tend to show wear more quickly. Tile cleans up easily with a damp sponge; for tougher dirt use a glass cleaner. Grout joints are susceptible to stains, so consider using a darker color for the grout than for the tile itself.

Laminate

Laminate is still the most widely used countertop surfacing material. Similar in construction to laminate plank floors, these affordably priced countertops are made from layers of plastic sheeting and particleboard bonded together under heat and pressure. Most laminate manufacturers offer a product line in which the color runs through the polymer sheet, eliminating the brown line often associated with edgings and making scratches and chips harder to see. The latest introductions have depth and look more like stone than ever before.

This porcelain tile floor (above) features a honed look that resembles travertine stone. As with stone, color runs through the entire thickness of solid-surfacing (left) so it can be shaped into a variety of edge treatments.

Recent introductions in laminate (above) do an excellent job of replicating natural stone. This granite look-alike has pitting slmilar to naturally aged stone.

The sand-tone quartz counter (above) mimics the look of honed natural stone. The shiny black quartz counter (left) resembles granite but was easler to install because it is much lighter in weight.

This rich, dark laminate (above) captures the look of cherry planks.

Wood countertops and floors (above) add a sense of warmth and age in keeping with this kitchen's vintage look. Wood can be stained and finished multiple times in a variety of colors and patterns to match any decor (left).

WOOD AND WOOD LOOK-ALIKES

Hardwood planks

The most familiar type of wood plank flooring is composed of solid, one-piece wood boards. A variety called "engineered" wood flooring consists of two or more layers of wood laminated together, similar to plywood. The top layers consist of a hardwood veneer; the bottom layers are typically made from softer woods. Both engineered and solid woods are wear-resistant, and they provide a naturally warm look. Because wood is not as hard as ceramic or stone, it is more comfortable to walk on.

Laminate

Slightly less expensive than wood, laminate plank flooring looks and feels similar to traditional wood but can be installed over existing flooring. It is durable and easy to take care of, but it can't be refinished like traditional wood planks. Laminate tiles, made to resemble stone, are also available.

Bamboo

Technically a grass, not wood, bamboo is harder than maple or oak and grows much more quickly, making it an earth-friendly choice.

Wood counters

Wood counters are attractive, versatile, and easier to care for than you might think. When sealed with a marine-quality polyurethane, the material can withstand occasional moisture but should be wiped dry as soon as possible. Regular polishing ensures a lasting finish.

This maple-topped island (above) is flanked by two heart-pine columns, which provide needed structural support. The bamboo used for flooring (below) matures in just three years, making it an excellent choice for the environmentally conscious.

COMFORT UNDERFOOT

Vinyl

This resilient floor covering is flexible, water- and stain-resistant, and easy to maintain. Because the flooring is relatively soft, it helps muffle noise and is easy on the feet and legs. Its drawback is that it can dent, and sharp knives may cut through the surface.

Linoleum

Made from organic materials, linoleum is known for its bright colors and long wear. Extremely popular in the 1950s, it is staging a comeback thanks to its earth-friendly, nonallergenic nature.

Cork

This natural flooring material is also returning to popularity—it is comfortable underfoot, environmentally friendly, and easy to care for.

Cork flooring is available in tiles (above) or sheets in a variety of colors and subtle patterns.

Linoleum tiles bring a nostalgic look to this new kitchen floor (above).

Glass Panache

Sleek and ever stylish, glass surfaces are becoming a popular choice in the kitchen.

Glass tiles are popular because of their easy care, sparkle, array of colors, and translucent beauty. These clear tiles (above left) lend a translucent quality to the kitchen's backsplash. Glass-block backsplashes (above center) open a kitchen to sunlight without relinquishing privacy or storage space. They are ideal where the view is less than perfect or in interior installations where additional sunlight can filter in from adjoining exterior spaces. Glass counters (above right) lend a look of sophistication to any kitchen. This counter features a clear top and a textured bottom layer that helps mask scratches.

Affordable vinyl tiles come in dozens of colors that inspire custom designs—although this black-and-white checkerboard is a kitchen classic. The material is also available in sheet form.

A stainless-steel counter and backsplash (above) perfectly match the professional range and vent hood. Concrete floors and counters bring an industrial look to this kitchen (right).

TRENDSETTERS

Concrete is tough enough to pave highways, so it's no wonder that it's becoming a popular hard-wearing surfacing material for the home. Easy to clean and versatile, concrete mimics the look of stone at a lower cost. Although it always has a rough-hewn quality, it can be colored, scored, and textured to create many interesting looks. Before it is fully cured, concrete can be stamped to create additional texture, and decorative tiles and metals can be inlaid for a custom look. Because concrete is very porous, it must be sealed for protection against embedded dirt and stains.

Metals are a stylish choice for counters, backsplashes, and even cabinetry. Stainless steel is the most popular because it is easy to clean and adds sleek texture that harmonizes with appliances. Copper, brass, and other metals can also be used but typically require additional care and sealing treatments.

Synthetic lavastone is shiny, nearly as durable as granite, and available in an array of colors from bright reds and stark whites to deep black and dark blues.

Shiny lavastone counters (above) will not stain like white marble.

Left untreated, copper counters evolve and change color over time. This counter (above) was sealed with a special coating so that it will maintain its shiny-penny color. Mosaic stainless-steel tiles give this backsplash (left) plenty of texture and shine.

Surfaces at a Glance

MATERIAL	PROS	CONS	COST
Stone	• Virtually indestructible • Elegant • Some varieties, such as granite, require little or no maintenance. • Impervious to heat • Cool surface is ideal for rolling out pastry.	• Expensive • Some varieties, such as marble and limestone, readily absorb stains and dirt. • Difficult to repair • Dark, glossy surfaces show fingerprints. • Some varieties require sealing periodically.	$100–$300 per running foot for slabs $3–$30 per square foot installed for tiles
Quartz (engineered stone) surfacing	• Durable • Wider range of colors than stone • Does not require sealing	• Uniform look doesn't mimic natural look of stone. • Edges may chip. • Intense heat can damage the surface.	$50–$100 per square foot installed
Solid-surfacing	• Requires little maintenance • Scratches, abrasions, and minor burns can be repaired with fine-grade sandpaper. • Available in many colors • Sinks can be integrated directly into the countertop.	• Intense heat and heavy falling objects can cause damage. • Can be scratched	$100–$250 per linear foot installed
Ceramic tile	• Durable • Water- and stain- resistant • Wide choice of colors, designs, textures, and shapes	• Grout lines can be hard to clean. • Lower quality tiles may chip. • Fragile items dropped on the surface probably will break. • Glossy tiles can be slippery when wet. • Difficult to repair	Counters: $18–$140 per linear foot installed Floors: $3–$12 per square foot installed
Laminate	• Durable, affordable • Easy to clean and maintain • Resists moisture and stains • Wide range of colors and designs • New introductions resemble natural materials.	• Can be scratched • Cannot be refinished if damaged	Counters: $26–$60 per linear foot installed Floors: $2–$9 per square foot installed
Wood	• Wear-resistant • Long-lasting • Provides a warm look • Can be refinished	• Vulnerable to moisture • Softer woods, such as pine, may dent easily. • May darken with age • Some finishes wear unevenly and are difficult to repair. • Can shrink and expand, creating gaps or warping	Counters: $50–$100 per linear foot installed Floors: $6–$14 per square foot installed

Surfaces at a Glance

MATERIAL	PROS	CONS	COST
Engineered wood	• Shrinks and expands less than wood • Resists moisture and spills • Installs over many substrates	• Typically can be refinished only once • Shows wear faster than solid wood	$4–$11 per square foot
Bamboo	• More quickly renewable resource than wood • Strong	• May darken or fade when exposed to sunlight • Should not be left wet	$5–$7 per square foot
Vinyl	• Durable • Water-resistant in sheet form • Easy to clean • Comfortable • Less expensive than most flooring choices	• Difficult to repair • Less expensive grades may discolor. • In tile form, moisture can get into seams between tiles.	$1–$5 per square foot
Linoleum	• Made of natural raw materials • More durable than vinyl • Color extends through entire material.	• Should be resealed annually • Cannot be left wet	$4–$9 per square foot
Cork	• Soft and warm, natural • Resists mildew • Does not absorb water • Sleek, contemporary look • Stain- and water-resistant • Easy to clean	• Finish must be sanded off and reapplied every few years	$4–$9 per square foot installed
Glass	• Sleek, contemporary look • Stain- and water-resistant • Easy to clean	• Can scratch • Cannot be repaired • Heavy falling objects can shatter surface. • Shows water spots and fingerprints	$200–$250 per square foot installed
Stainless steel	• Durable • Stain- and water-resistant	• Scratches easily • Shiny finishes show water spots and fingerprints.	$50–$75 per square foot
Lavastone	• Virtually indestructible • Elegant • Requires little or no maintenance • Impervious to heat	• Expensive • Difficult to repair • Dark, glossy surfaces show fingerprints.	$500 or more per square foot installed

DESIGN GALLERY
Material Mix

With an ever-increasing array of material choices, selecting the right mix can be a daunting task. These sound selection strategies will help you strike the right balance of finishes.

1. To prevent sensory overload in a brightly colored kitchen, choose simple materials for countertops and floors. Wood plank floors and gray-green marble counters let chartreuse cabinets take center stage.

2. For a warm and woodsy ambience, choose a combination of natural materials. Gray slate backsplash tiles, dark pine cabinets, and oak floors work well in this Rocky Mountain retreat. A red stained island and red accent tiles add contrast.

3. Neutral color schemes keep your kitchen's design focus on architectural details and textural differences. Smooth natural maple cabinets combine with sand-color honed limestone floors and a rough-cut limestone wall. Contrast comes from the shiny black granite tile counter.

4. Bring interest to a white-cabinet kitchen with contrasting surface colors. Creamy white glazed cabinets combine with a gray-blue granite countertop and blue-and-white tile accents and accessories.

5. Warm a sleek kitchen with brightly stained accent cabinets and upholstered chairs.

One kitchen wall consolidates all the oven options a family or passionate cook might need—a double oven, a microwave, a toaster oven, and a warming drawer. A deep, double-basin sink and high-arc faucet (opposite) ease food preparation and cleanup chores.

CHAPTER 6

Appliances, Sinks & Faucets

Cooling and cooking food with efficiency and cleaning up effectively begin when you make smart choices for these critical kitchen components.

Equipping your kitchen with the right appliances, sinks, and faucets helps you save time, eat healthfully, and perform like a pro. When you shop for appliances, consider these points:

Read the manual before you buy. Most manufacturers have their appliance manuals posted on their websites. Browse through them to learn about features and capabilities.

Check efficiency. New advances could save you money. For example a dishwasher with low energy consumption, a delay timer, and an economy cycle or half-load button will result in saving water and money.

Recognize the benefits of point-of-use appliances. Appliance drawers—for warming food, washing dishes, and cooling food—can make your kitchen more efficient and flexible. Undercounter refrigerators, for example, put produce where you prepare meals.

Focus on features. Shop around to get a feel for the available features. Then zero in on those that are important to you.

Although this separate refrigerator and freezer are substantial, the built-in appliances feature cherry panel fronts that allow them to blend into the kitchen setting.

REFRIGERATION

With refrigerators the main question is where you want the freezer compartment. Though top-mount units (freezer on the top) are most common, a bottom-mount model may be easier on your body. "If you have the refrigerator in the middle range—from the knees to the shoulders—with the freezer below, it's actually the most ergonomic," says St. Louis kitchen designer Chris Berry.

Side-by-sides

Side-by-side models lack appeal, Berry says, because of their narrow compartments. "The only nice thing about a side-by-side is ice and water dispensing in the door," she says. "But unless it's at least 42 inches wide, the freezer becomes worthless in a side-by-side."

Diane Ebeling, a certified kitchen designer in Boulder, Colorado, likes units that have two compressors—one for the refrigerator and one for the freezer. "You don't have air transferring back and forth, so your ice doesn't taste like last night's fish," Ebeling says. She names tight door seals, climate-controlled bins, and adjustable shelves as other key refrigerator features.

Built-Ins

Built-in refrigerators, especially those with cabinetry-matching panels, create a clean look. "The only advantage to not doing a built-in appliance is cost," says Matthew Rao, a certified kitchen designer in Atlanta. Of course, he concedes, it is a big advantage: You could pay $600 for a freestanding refrigerator and $6,000 for a built-in.

Drawers

For maximum cold-storage flexibility, consider augmenting your full-size refrigerator/freezer with point-of-use refrigerator and freezer drawers, a small undercounter fridge, a wine refrigerator, or a separate icemaker. Refrigerated or freezer drawers can be handy when near a secondary workstation. Or place them near the breakfast table so family members can grab snacks without interrupting the work core.

Designing this kitchen (above) sans upper cabinets and a massive refrigerator keeps the look airy. Banks of appliance drawers—including these refrigerated ones—ensure ultimate function without the bulk.

Buying Tips

The biggest refrigerator on the planet is useless if you can't find what you need. Look for bins, racks, and shelves that tilt, lift, or subdivide to organize everything from deli trays to yogurt cups.

Follow these pointers when looking for a new refrigerator:

• Know your measurements. Standard refrigerators protrude beyond standard (24-inch-deep) cabinets. You can ensure a streamlined look by buying a counter-depth (also called cabinet-depth) refrigerator, available as a built-in or freestanding unit. Be prepared for a jump in price of several hundred dollars for this feature.

• Opinions differ when it comes to through-the-door dispensers for ice and water. They are convenient but perhaps too handy for kids who don't bother to pick up stray ice cubes. Also, they eliminate energy lost from opening the door, but cleaning the doors takes more than a swipe. Talk to friends who have dispensers before you buy. (Note: Manufacturers are starting to include this feature on French-door refrigerators.)

• Although many freestanding refrigerators come in stainless steel (or a stainless-steel look-alike) for the effect of a high-end built-in model, typically only the doors are stainless steel; the sides are black.

A professional-grade range, such as this one, tops the wish list of many dedicated cooks thanks to its durability, high-Btu gas burners, and classic appearance.

OVENS, RANGES, & COOKTOPS

A big decision here is whether to buy a range—combined cooktop and oven(s)—or a cooktop and separate ovens.

Cooktops

Diane Ebeling says stand-alone cooktops are a good fit for clean, contemporary kitchens, while full ranges make sense in small kitchens, especially when there is limited space for wall ovens.

Matthew Rao recommends an induction cooktop on an island as a cool design—in more ways than one. "It makes a lot of sense because it doesn't create heat that stays trapped in the unit," he says. And if you're a serious cook and entertainer, he adds, pair that cooktop with a convection oven.

Buying Tips

Stainless steel, oversize knobs, and other commercial influences permeate most categories and price levels of ranges, cooktops, and ovens. But you may prefer a retro model or European looks such as mirror glass, rich color, or minimalism. In addition to the standard 30-inch-wide range or oven you can now find sizes from 24 to 60 inches—the better to fit your kitchen layout.

Ecologically and financially it pays to invest in energy-efficient appliances. When you prepare a meal faster, you use less gas or electricity, and food that is steamed or speed-cooked can taste better and be better for you.

For two people a convection microwave oven and a two-burner cooktop may suffice. Conversely double ovens and six-burner ranges are a boon to big families and frequent entertainers. Today's appliance options let you customize your kitchen to work for you.

When shopping for a cooking appliance, consider these points:

• A professional-grade range (48 inches or wider) may need special planning to install. Check the weight and ask a contractor if your floor needs reinforcing. Plan for ventilation designed for a professional-grade range, and leave installation to a professional.

• If your budget allows, a double oven will help you bake in quantity. It's wise to consider at least one cavity with convection mode. Keep in mind, though, that you'll lose the flexibility of placing individual ovens below counter height.

• When you compare gas cooktops, look for continuous burner grates. They create a uniform and stable cooking platform that lets you slide pans across the surface without fear they'll tip or wobble.

• The more you have, the more you want. The trend in stove tops is more burners. But before you buy, make sure the stove has adequate space between burners for simultaneous cooking.

A small steam oven (below the built-in coffeemaker) requires little wall space and adds healthy cooking convenience.

Whatever kind of cooktop you choose, says Chris Berry, don't limit yourself to four burners. "There are so many times when the fifth or sixth burner makes a lot of sense," she says. "So for the extra 6 inches difference in width between a 30-inch, four-burner range and a 36-inch, five- or six-burner range, you get more bang for your buck, and there's not much difference in price."

Carlene Anderson, a certified kitchen designer in Oakland, says to consider which cooking appliances are easiest to use—and to clean. "What I tell clients is to imagine they're putting on a great big pasta feed and the sauce is flying all over the place, and at the last minute, they decide to saute some eggplant," she says. "Then after everybody's gone home, look at the range or cooktop—it needs to be cleaned."

Economy versus professional

So what's the difference between economy models and the professional-grade units? With cooktops, Anderson says, there is a big difference in the quality of burners and the amount of heat they can generate, but that might be all.

"Basically when you strip all these appliances of their grates, knobs, handles, and everything, sometimes some of the internal workings aren't that different, and

These two sets of stacked ovens are separated—a smart configuration for multiple bakers.

the food doesn't know the difference," Anderson says. "It's really a question of the ergonomics of touching it, turning it on, and how easy it is to clean up."

Anderson prefers open burners to sealed burners because they get more oxygen to the fuel, yet they're still easy to clean. And whether you prefer a cooktop or a range, she says it's nice to have the controls on the front of the unit, not on the back, to avoid having to reach over hot burners.

Ovens and cookware

As for types of ovens you should consider, Anderson pronounces a clear preference. "I've never cooked anything that wasn't better in a convection oven," she says.

Lastly, make sure your new cooktop or oven works with your cookware. "Know the sizes of your pots and pans and baking sheets before you go out looking," Ebeling says. Take a favorite skillet or stockpot along on shopping trips to test burner spacing.

Cooking Advances

You have more cooking choices than ever. Here are some of the latest innovations:

Steam ovens. Considered one of the most healthful methods of preparing food, steam cooking has until recently been left to the pros. But an increasing number of appliance manufacturers have entered the market, making it easy to prepare moist, flavorful foods at home. Most steam ovens do not require special plumbing.

Speed ovens. These appliances cook as much as 75 percent faster than conventional ovens, owing their speed to various combinations of microwave, convection, and quartz-halogen cooking. Due to its size and specialty, a speed oven makes a good second oven. No need to adapt recipes; most models will adjust cooking times and temperatures for you.

Induction cooking. Enjoying renewed interest, induction cooking offers rapid heat-up and cooldown similar to that offered by gas, but its temperature is easier to control. Induction cooking is also considered safer: A magnetic field heats the food inside pans quickly while the surface of the burners stays relatively cool.

Stacked wall ovens team with this dual-oven range to provide multiple baking options in this kitchen.

Ventilation Hoods

Range hoods have come a long way since the days when they were considered purely functional elements. They still have to ventilate heat and odors, but today's models prove beauty can go hand in hand with function. According to the Home Ventilating Institute, a range hood should be at least the same width as the cooking surface it serves and mounted directly over it, 18 to 30 inches above the burners.

DISHWASHERS

In today's most efficient kitchens, the ideal dishwasher is neither seen nor heard. Sleek exteriors and sophisticated hidden controls have rendered many models nearly invisible, while sound-deadening features have made them quieter than ever.

Interior options can increase the cost of a dishwasher, but some are worth it. Stainless-steel interiors, for example, are more durable than enamel finishes, which may chip and rust. Heavy-duty racks, removable and adjustable, handle the biggest pots. Other features to consider are built-in water softeners, water-temperature boosters, interior lights, special cycles, hidden controls, and doors ready for cabinetry-matching panels.

"They all deliver a clean plate," says kitchen designer Carlene Anderson. "It just depends on which rack system you like." She prefers a unit without a visible control panel. "It's one less thing to clean," she says. Pay for quality, Anderson says, but don't go overboard on features. "Very few people put their crystal in there or use all the different buttons," she says. "I push the same button every night."

If you have a large household or do a lot of entertaining, you may get more benefit from two economical dishwashers than one top-of-the-line model

Dishwasher drawers are another option, especially in kitchens where the size of loads is small or tends to vary. "You either love them or hate them," interior designer Chris Berry says of the drawers. "You cannot put a cookie sheet, a big stockpot, or an asparagus steamer in a dishwasher drawer. For me that would be personal hell because if it doesn't go in the dishwasher, it doesn't get washed."

Buying Tips: Dishwashers

Big loads or small, washing casseroles or crystal, new dishwashers are smarter and quieter than before. Even if you shopped only a few years ago, you'll find innovation on all fronts. Take loading options, where adjustable racks, removable tines, and stemware holders keep any mix of items in place while getting them sparkling clean. And you can finally break that prerinsing habit—multiple arms, built-in heaters, and targeted sprays get everything the first time. But perhaps the most progress has been made environmentally. Like laundry equipment, dishwashers have become misers with electricity, water, and sound. Most manufacturers sell several models that meet or exceed Energy Star guidelines, so even if the prices seem higher, you'll save on utility costs for years to come. As of January 2007, Energy Star-rated dishwashers must be a minimum of 41 percent more efficient than federal energy standards. This requirement is up from 25 percent.

Here are some things to keep in mind when shopping for a dishwasher:

• For a streamlined look, choose a unit with electronic controls integrated into the top edge of the door. Although only visible when the door is ajar, these controls are at an angle some people find easier to read than the front-facing position of typical controls. Look for hidden controls on a unit that accepts a cabinet panel to make the dishwasher practically disappear.

• Models that boast ultraquiet performance have been the focus of introductions in the past few years. Some manufacturers of hidden-control units have incorporated a visible light so customers can tell when the dishwasher is on, even when they can't hear it.

• Although the compact drawer design is a popular option, make sure it fits your household needs. Many drawer systems hold up to five place settings, but if you have a large family or entertain quite often, a standard model may be better. If you are still hooked on the idea of a drawer model, make sure to plan for two-drawer systems in your kitchen workspace.

SINKS AND FAUCETS

Sinks and faucets may be the most hardworking kitchen elements, but they can also be attractive. With so many options available, you can easily find the right blend of style and function. The key is to look at the sink and faucet as a team and shop accordingly.

When looking for a sink, consider size, shape, and material. How many bowls do you need? Is

Two dishwashers (above) flank the sink to handle cleanups for a family or party. Installing a pot filler (below right) above the range top eases cooking chores.

Buying Tips: Faucets

Sleek and contemporary or ornate and traditional, faucets contribute largely to a kitchen's overall style and can influence the look of such elements as cabinetry hardware. In addition to a variety of main-sink faucets, you'll find scaled-down bar and prep-sink faucets, filtered-water faucets, electronic models, and instant-hot and -cold faucets. Pull-down models are considered more ergonomic than pullouts and often feature restaurant style. The hottest trend is a pot-filler faucet, typically mounted near the range, that delivers cold water only and eliminates hauling a pot of water from the sink.

Consider these tips when looking for a kitchen faucet:

• Choose the best you can afford. Kitchen faucets get daily use and are worth the extra investment.

• Test drive before you buy. Make sure the spout and handles or levers are easy to work and that the sprayer pulls out and returns easily.

• Study your sink. A too-tall faucet for the sink depth can create splashes; too low can limit the amount of clearance for filling large pots. If your sink is predrilled, be sure to check its number of faucet holes so the faucet you choose will fit.

the sink deep enough for your biggest pots? Today's technology has made many materials equal in durability, letting cost and style drive choices. In addition to stainless steel and cast iron, options include copper, slate, marble, granite, soapstone, and stone composites.

Besides enhancing your sink's style, the faucet must have a spout long enough to reach all the bowls and high enough to allow clearance for your tallest cookware.

Spending the additional dollars for an upgraded faucet not only provides a richer look but also makes many chores more convenient. Pullout sprayer hoses up to 59 inches long are ideal for rinsing large dishes as well as for tasks such as dog bathing and plant watering.

If you equate convenience with luxury, join the pasta lovers and soup makers who swear by wallmount faucets plumbed in over a range for filling stockpots. Look for faucets that extend 20 to 26 inches from the wall.

Sink Material Pros and Cons

MATERIAL	PROS	CONS
Cast iron Molten iron is poured into a mold and a durable enamel coating is fired on for color and shine.	These sinks produce minimal noise and vibration, and hold water temperature for long periods.	Cast-iron sinks can be extremely heavy, and the enamel coating can scratch and discolor.
Composite Every company seems to have its own recipe for composite material. Whether a sink is made of quartz, granite, or other materials mixed with a resin base, it usually features beautiful speckled color.	They're resistant to stains, dents, and scratches and are easy-care; just don't use an abrasive cleanser.	Buy the best you can afford. Composite sinks with higher ratios of resin fillers may not be as durable and stain-resistant as those with higher ratios of quartz or granite.
Fireclay A clay base is fired to produce a durable, glossy finish. Some makers offer beautiful but pricey sinks with fired, painted designs.	The glazed surface resists scratches, rust, and fading.	Fireclay is somewhat porous and can stain over time.
Solid-surfacing Solid-surfacing consists of a polyester or acrylic base with different ingredients used by each manufacturer. Although many manufacturers offer ready-made models, solid-surfacing is known for its custom applications.	Known for its easy care and stonelike beauty, it is available in a range of colors and resists scratches and chips. Color runs through the material, so minor burns or scrapes can be sanded out. Solid-surfacing sinks are often integrated with a solid-surfacing countertop for a seamless and easy-to-clean setup with no sink lip to catch crumbs.	Solid-surfacing can be nearly as expensive as granite, and though it is resistant to chips, it is not completely damage-proof.
Stainless steel A new generation of 16- and 18-gauge stainless-steel sinks is thicker and less noisy than the predecessors. Stainless-steel sinks contain a percentage of chromium and nickel, indicated by numbers such as 18/10 (18 percent chromium and 10 percent nickel). Choose from various finishes, such as a mirrorlike shine or a satin luster.	The metals are corrosion resistant and impart a rich glow to kitchen decor.	Stainless steel does scratch, and the thinner, less durable grades (such as a 21-gauge sink) can be noisy with running water and clattering dishes.
Vitreous china This material is clay coated with a fired-on glaze. It is similar to fireclay in construction, durability, and cost but is less porous than fireclay.	Hard and nonporous, vitreous china boasts a glasslike shine.	The nature of the construction process makes it more difficult to mold double-bowl kitchen sinks out of vitreous china than fireclay.

Kitchen Product Price Guide

APPLIANCE	BUDGET	BETTER	SPLURGE
Range	$300–$550 • Painted cabinet; conventional gas or electric burners; oven window	$500–$3,000 • Large (up to 12,000 Btus) gas, glass-top electric, or induction burners; programmable convection oven; stainless-steel front panel	$1,300–$10,000+ • Dual-fuel models with burners that range from 500 to 15,000 Btus; stainless-steel cabinets; convection ovens; commercial-grade; vintage styles
Range vent hood and light	$80–$400 • 180–350 cubic feet per minute (cfm) air movement; 30–36 inches wide	$500–$1,400 • Up to 700 cfm; widths to 48 inches; larger filter area; optional stainless-steel chimney hood; halogen lamps; quiet operation	$1,200–$5,000+ • Up to 1,200 cfm; 60-inch widths; halogen lamps; dishwasher-safe, baffle-type grease traps; curved-glass canopies; custom-built
Wall oven	$400–$900 • 27-inch single unit; dial controls; limited finishes	$750–$2,000 • 30-inch single oven with convection or double oven without convection; digital/touch-pad controls; programmable; finish choices including stainless steel	$1,600–$5,000+ • Stainless-steel or painted finishes; European-type convection; digital controls; halogen lights; heavy-duty racks; stacked double units
Refrigerator/ freezer	$500–$800 • Wire shelves; icemaker option; finish choices: white, almond, biscuit, black	$800–$3,300 • Large-capacity side-by-side or bottom-freezer model; independent temperature-control zones; through-the-door ice and water dispenser; stainless steel	$3,500–$7,000+ • Luxury built-in (flush with cabinetry); stainless-steel housing or customized front panels to match cabinetry; widths 24–60 inches
Dishwasher	$300–$525 • Two-rack model; plastic interior; several wash cycles; push-button/dial controls; color choices: white, black, almond, biscuit	$650–$900 • Stainless-steel interior; touch-pad controls; quiet operation; three racks or modular loading areas; more cycle options	$900–$2,200 • Heat boosters; front-panel customization; better tub; ultraquiet
Kitchen sink and faucet	$110–$330 • Thin-wall stainless steel or white enamel on steel; twin basin self-rimming; single- or two-handle faucet with polished-chrome finish	$350–$1,400 • Porcelain or cast iron, colored enamel; two or three basins; faucet in finish choice	$1,000–$5,000+ • Undermount, apron-front sink in heavy-gauge stainless steel, copper, stone, or engineered granite; sink accessories for food prep and cleanup; designer finishes

DESIGN GALLERY
Something Extra

There's more to the kitchen appliance scene than refrigerators, ranges, dishwashers, and the like. Consider the benefits of bringing a "fringe" appliance or two into your plans. These are just a few options.

1. A flat-panel television screen mounted on the wall entertains you while you work.

2. A warming drawer keeps meals hot for diners who arrive late.

3. Keep wines at the perfect temperature in a special cooler.

4. A central vacuum lets you flip a switch and sweep dirt toward the floor-level outlet.

5. A built-in coffeemaker frees up counters and connects to the water supply.

CHAPTER 7

Lighting Your Kitchen

Lighting is often one of the last design features planned, but consider how important it is to illuminate every task as well as enjoy the lovely details.

A combination of fixtures and unobtrusive undercabinet lighting ensures that this kitchen (opposite and above) has ample illumination. During the day a wall of windows provides abundant natural light.

Lighting is one of the most subtle but critical elements in your kitchen, determining how it looks and functions. This is also the room in the house that presents the greatest lighting challenge: It's a functional space for activities that no one should do in the dark, such as wielding sharp utensils, cooking over hot burners, and handling glassware. You need a certain amount of lighting to prevent accidents and eyestrain.

A kitchen is also a place to gather in a relaxed atmosphere. Your family or guests don't want to sit at an island and feel as though they're being interrogated under a halogen spotlight.

With this range of needs, it's no wonder your kitchen requires varying kinds of lighting to illuminate the whole room, to focus on special tasks, and to create a mood. It also helps to put fixtures on dimmers: The same pendent light that lets you read a recipe can be dimmed when friends come for dinner. And lights (or groups of lights) can be turned off independently when not needed.

185

Pendants over the island and table (this photo and opposite) combine with track lighting for a contemporary scheme. Glass shades (left) repeat the wall color.

The Right Bulb for the Job

You'll find a bevy of bulb choices. Here are a few to consider:

Compact fluorescent: Chosen for long life and energy efficiency, these bulbs are booming in popularity and can screw into a variety of fixtures. According to the Environmental Protection Agency's Energy Star program, if every American home replaced just one lightbulb with a compact fluorescent lightbulb, or CFL, the energy savings would be equal to lighting more than 3 million homes for a year. On average you'll save about $30 or more in electricity costs over each bulb's lifetime.

The EPA recommends using reflector CFLs (rather than spirals) in recessed fixtures so that the light distributes more evenly. If the light fixture is connected to a dimmer or three-way switch, you'll need to use a special CFL designed to work in these applications. (Look for the specified use on the packaging.) Although most CFLs provide warm or soft white light, you should choose a cooler color for task lighting.

Halogen: In fixtures and lamps these bulbs provide clear white light. Do not use them in homes with small children; the bulbs get quite hot.

Incandescent: Classic for warm, soft light or for light tinted by colored bulbs, these easy-to-find bulbs are used for lamps and overhead fixtures.

Reflector: Designed for ceiling or wall track lighting and recessed fixtures, these coated bulbs provide directional light.

Three-way: Used for lamps with three-way switches, these bulbs are an easy way to create mood lighting without dimmers.

Xenon bulbs: New on the market, xenon is becoming popular for accent lighting and undercabinet lighting because it provides a clear white light. The bulbs are a variation of the halogen bulb but are cooler-burning and use less energy.

ALLOVER LIGHTING

In any good lighting scheme, your goal is to fill the room with well-blended layers of light—illuminating both what you need to see, such as a workspace, and what you want to see, such as sparkling glassware. General lighting is used to cast a comfortable level of brightness throughout the kitchen. It is best achieved with a mix of sources, such as a central ceiling-mounted fixture and recessed spotlights around the perimeter. Dark-color kitchens need more general lighting than bright-color ones. You'll also need more electric lighting during the day for a kitchen with fewer windows. To achieve adequate light levels using recessed can lights, allow one for every 20 to 25 square feet.

TASK LIGHTING

Intended to illuminate a task or a specific area, this bright light is work-oriented. To generate task lighting choose fixtures that focus the light onto one spot, such as small pendants or individual recessed cans over an island or sink.

Undercabinet lights serve as task lights for the countertop. Use slim fluorescent tubes or low-voltage halogen "hockey puck" lights, which can be hidden in the undercabinet recess. The fixtures are hardwired by an electrician at the front of the cabinet, not the back. Otherwise you're highlighting only the backsplash or causing glare, which can be noticeable if your countertops are polished stone instead of a honed or matte surface.

In a kitchen with no windows (above right), use recessed and task lighting fixtures to illuminate the cooktop and counters. Add lights inside the cabinets to cast a comforting glow. Install halogen pucks at the top of a glass-door cabinet (above) to make glassware sparkle. Glass shelves allow the light to flow throughout the display.

Accent Lighting

Lighting can also be used to set a mood:

• Uplighting is placed below its intended target and pointed up. Install fluorescent bulbs above your cabinets and let the light bounce off the ceiling to create a soft glow. Or uplight with wall sconces.

• For drama and beauty, highlight artwork or a collectible with a spotlight or a recessed ceiling fixture aimed toward the piece at a 30-degree angle. This type of accent lighting should be three times brighter than the surrounding lighting to be effective. Accent stemware and collectibles in glass-door cabinets with low-voltage halogen light for the best sparkle.

• Accent lighting can also be as simple as a group of candles on a tabletop or the glow of burning logs from a fireplace.

Pendant Position

For a right-height light, Bryan Janssen of Dent Electrical Supply in Danbury, Connecticut, recommends suspending the fixture so the bottom of the shade is about 28 inches above the work surface. A lower position may obstruct your view across the room, and anything higher can make the fixture seem disconnected. Janssen says halogen lamps give a crisp white light that shows off food colors; incandescent lamps, although warm-looking, make colors appear less bold. To set the mood for dining and entertaining, add a dimming control to the fixture.

In this kitchen thoughtfully positioned pendent fixtures bring light closer to the cooktop, the sink, and the countertop surface.

DESIGN GALLERY
Mood Makers

Employ creative lighting strategies to shape the atmosphere of your kitchen. Include accent lighting to bring out your kitchen's best features and to set the mood.

1. Sconces gently illuminate this alcove while lighting tucked on top of the molding radiates upward and onto the ceiling.

2. Dining always seems a little more romantic by firelight. This fireplace casts a soft glow that's as inviting as candlelight.

3. Table lamps top the storage console to provide radiance.

4. LED lighting inside a glass-front cabinet highlights objects with a crisp light.

The lowdown on LEDs

In the next few years, light-emitting diodes (LEDs) will have a major impact on residential lighting design. Although more expensive than fluorescent and incandescent bulbs, LEDs are extremely energy-efficient, and the technology is evolving swiftly.

"LEDs don't burn out suddenly like other bulbs," says designer Patricia Rizzo. "They just gradually fade away. Depending on how you use them, they can literally last a lifetime."

LEDs put out focused rather than general light, so bulbs are well-suited for task lighting. The light is typically white and crisp like halogen light, but the bulbs burn cooler. LEDs can also produce colored light.

The most successful kitchen renovations look as though they have always been a part of the home. This to-the-studs update (this page and opposite) appears original to the 1940s cottage.

CHAPTER 8

Realize Your Dream

Once you have decided how you want your kitchen
to function and look, it's time to get the project rolling.

before

There's no one-size-fits-all formula to determine the cost and the time frame needed for a kitchen update. Many factors affect price and completion time, including the size of your project, the materials and features you want, and the laborers you hire. Local codes, the location of your home, and fluctuations in material costs affect the design and construction—and therefore cost—of your renovation. An addition in Wisconsin, for example, will be significantly cheaper than the same changes in San Francisco, a city known for its strict building codes. Be aware of potential expenses before you build to avoid heartache when you see the final price tag.

THE CONSTRUCTION PROCESS

The kitchen renovation process involves five stages: planning, budgeting, demolition, construction, and cleanup. Make the right decisions at each step and you'll finish your project on time and on budget.

Planning

List and prioritize your wants and needs, then stick with your plan to avoid unexpected costs or delays. Even small changes, such as a different faucet, a doorknob, or flooring material, can cause major problems, especially if items must be reordered and subcontractors rescheduled.

Budgeting

Ask at least two general contractors and kitchen designers or architects for estimates. Many offer this service free. Talk with friends to see how much they spent for similar projects, but keep in mind that location and material prices can make a difference.

Designers and architects charge 5 to 15 percent of the total project budget. Although you may be tempted to avoid this expense, remember that professionals can save you money in the long run and ensure the aesthetic result you desire. They offer expert advice on design options and products, can catch problems experienced

To-the-studs renovations like this one (left) often take as much time as additions because contractors must work around existing supports and plumbing and electrical lines.

before

A makeover need not be costly. A new cherry-color finish (left) gives these oak cabinets (above) a fresh look. Granite tiles update the counters.

Natural Order

If you are building a kitchen addition, the foundation and framing go up first with windows to follow. After that come the plumbing, wiring, and heating and cooling (if any). Insulation, drywall, roofing, and siding complete the shell. Inside, finish carpentry, electrical connections, and flooring follow. Appliances and lighting and plumbing fixtures are then installed. If your kitchen has a wood floor, it's sanded, stained, and sealed as the last step.

contractors miss, and tend to get more competitive bids from contractors. Expect an even better rate if a firm provides both design and building services. Always ask for formal and detailed bids as well as proof of licensing and references from professionals.

Demolition

If you have a few carpentry skills, you can save money by doing this yourself. Although it's tedious and hard work to remove elements such as walls, wiring, and carpet, you'll be rewarded with a lower total cost. Make sure to take breakables off the walls and cover or move furniture to protect it from dust and debris. This stage may be shorter than construction, but just as unsettling to daily life. For safety's sake, if you are uncertain of your abilities, hire a professional.

Construction

For larger projects consider temporarily moving out of your house, especially if you will lose electricity, heat, or water for a while. Compare prices for hotels, extended-stay hotels, apartments, or rental houses, depending on how long construction will take.

Cleanup

Your new space is almost ready, but before you can enjoy it, someone has to remove the dust and debris from construction. Although this is a labor-intensive project, you'll save money by doing some of it yourself.

To make a newly renovated room like this one (opposite) look as though it has always been a part of your home, take care to match window styles, woodwork, and interior door styles to those found elsewhere in the house.

Earth-Friendly Choices

Whether you are giving your kitchen a simple facelift or a down-to-the-studs makeover, you may need to dispose of appliances and materials. Items such as flooring, cabinetry, lighting, shelving, sinks, and tiles often can be salvaged and donated to organizations that resell them at a deep discount. Look in the Yellow Pages under "Building Materials–Used" or check with your local chapter of Habitat for Humanity to see whether it operates a ReStore.

If your old appliances are operable, call local charities to find out whether they will accept them. For nonworking appliances, ask the dealer where you are purchasing your new ones whether they will recycle your old ones.

If you add architectural features, such as clerestory windows, match the trimwork and mullions to the existing style.

Avoiding Unexpected Expenses

Request lien waivers. This documentation will release you from financial responsibility for a contractor's purchase of materials. Otherwise, if a contractor goes out of business, an unpaid supplier could place a claim on your property for the materials the contractor used. If you don't pay for the materials, the claim may complicate selling your house in the future.

Have your finances in order. Paying from savings is ideal but not possible for most people. Experts recommend home equity loans (which let you borrow against your home's value, minus the amount you owe on your mortgage) or lines of credit (the interest on which is deductible) over borrowing against 401(k) retirement plans, whole-term insurance policies, or other assets. A home-equity line of credit is the same as a loan, except you don't have to draw the full amount at any given time. Consult a financial planner for recommendations specific to your situation.

Be ready for surprises. Anything can happen when you start building, and every roadblock has its price. Maybe a small plumbing leak leads to removing a section of water-damaged subfloor. Maybe you realize that you don't have time to finish interior work after all and hire someone to do it. Budget at least a 20 percent margin for unexpected expenses.

Avoid going overboard. Nobody wants the most expensive house on the block—or the least expensive. Make sure your wish list is comparable to homes in your neighborhood; a costly addition may put your home out of the price range of potential buyers. Stick with your original plan to stay within limits. A few changes along the way are OK, but they'll likely increase the budget.

Recovering Remodeling Costs

Projects are listed in order of the amount of expected return on your investment.

PROJECT TYPE	AVERAGE COST OF PROJECT	AVERAGE RECOVERY COST	PERCENTAGE RECOUPED
Kitchen remodeling (minor)	$15,273	$14,195	92.9%
Kitchen remodeling (major, upscale)	$75,206	$60,367	80.3%
Kitchen remodeling (major, midrange)	$42,660	$33,890	79.4%

Keeping the basic layout and existing windows in this kitchen provided room in the budget for custom cabinetry and tile counters.

before

HIRING CONTRACTORS

Choose the right professionals

Too many homeowners make the mistake of hiring remodelers based solely on price. Ultimately the least expensive remodeler is not the one with the lowest bid but the one you trust with your checkbook.

To pick the best remodeler for you, ask friends and colleagues for suggestions. For local referrals contact a professional organization, such as the American Institute of Architects (AIA) (800/242-3837, www.aia.org) or the National Association of Home Builders (NAHB) (800/368-5242, www.nahb.org).

Talk with a remodeler's former clients and interview each remodeler personally to ensure you will feel comfortable working with him or her. The National Association of the Remodeling Industry (NARI) provides suggested interview questions on its website at www.nari.org. Click on "Homeowners," then "Interview Remodeler." Once you have a list of favorites, ask to tour some of their finished projects. Savvy architects and contractors will ask you questions as well to find out your expectations and needs. You should come away from each tour with an idea of the quality of their work and how well your personalities and visions for the project jibe.

To narrow your decision between the last two or three professionals, it may be worth the cost to solicit preliminary drawings from each one. This is a good way to test your working relationship and to land options from which to choose. In addition, ask contractors for bids. Don't base your decision on cost alone; rather, weigh what you learned in the interview with the thoroughness of the bid itself.

Be sure to have the facts on paper to protect you legally

Requesting Bids

These straightforward remodeling strategies can help you finish your project on time and on budget:

Plan, plan, plan. List and prioritize your remodeling needs and desires on paper. This ranking will help you make decisions when it comes to trimming the budget: Dropping the price becomes a matter of striking items from the bottom of the list. Share your ranking with the professionals you plan to work with so they will know what matters most to you.

Negotiate the details. If you have a few carpentry skills, you can reduce the overall cost of your remodeling project by doing some work yourself. Most contractors let homeowners do the tear-out. Although it's tedious and hard work to remove elements such as cabinets and floorings, you'll be rewarded with a lower total cost. When your new space is almost ready, someone will also have to remove the dust and debris from construction. Although this is also labor-intensive, you'll save money doing it yourself.

Request detailed estimates. Request bids with set prices, not ones that fluctuate based on the time and materials chosen. Be prepared to pay the professional's hourly rate for preparing this formal, detailed contract.

Note that remodelers often list items such as fixtures and appliances in contracts as allowances. A remodeler may calculate $500 for a dishwasher, for instance, or $1,000 for a range. Before agreeing to the contract, review the allowances carefully. Head to home centers, appliance stores, and surfacing retailers to see if the allowances are in line with your selections. If not, you'll need to renegotiate the bottom line or decide where you can save and where you'll want to splurge. If necessary, consider making improvements in phases, such as keeping your appliances for now and upgrading them in a few years. The time to make changes to your remodeling plan is now, not after the project starts.

Follow the plan. Once you have negotiated the details and have the costs on paper, stick to your plans. Even small changes, such as choosing a different sink or light fixture, can affect the bottom line, especially if materials have to be reordered and subcontractors rescheduled.

Sleek, pale maple cabinets give this condo kitchen contemporary flair and make the small room seem more spacious.

before, during, and after the work is done. Define the scope of the project and fees as specifically as possible. The contract should include a clear description of the work to be done, materials that will be required, and who will supply them. It should also spell out commencement and completion dates and any provisions relating to timeliness. It should list your total costs (subject to additions and deductions by a written change order only). Payments should be tied to work stages; be wary of any contractor who wants a lot of money up front. If certain materials need to be ordered weeks in advance (to allow time for manufacturing), get a list of them and their costs before committing to the idea of up-front money. Custom cabinets and professional-grade appliances may require a sizable cash advance.

Follow the law

Your remodeling plans must be within the confines of the law; otherwise you may be required to make costly modifications. Before you start any remodeling project, check your local building codes and ordinances. Most cities, towns, and municipalities have rules that determine where and what you can build. Although several kinds of local ordinances cover various aspects of the remodeling process, probably the most important are zoning regulations, setbacks, and easements.

Zoning restrictions typically affect additions. These regulations are designed to ensure that your plans will not adversely affect neighboring properties. Zoning regulations cover four basic building issues: height, width, use, and density. These rules specify the maximum height of a building; the width and depth of the building; its allowable uses, which include residential, commercial, industrial, and home-office considerations; and the number of units allowed per acre. Height and width are the two zoning restrictions that affect additions. If you want to add on to your kitchen, use considerations will probably not affect you. These restrictions are typically used to regulate home-based businesses.

Zoning Change

To keep up with technology and the changing needs of a community, zoning regulations are modified periodically. Therefore, if you live in an older neighborhood, your home may not be consistent with the zone where you live. For example, you may have a single-family home in a commercial or multifamily zone. This is known as preexisting, nonconforming use. In this instance any addition to your home will need approval from the municipality in which you live. This approval, called a variance, permits an exception to the rules for your specific situation. In some municipalities achieving approval for a variance is a long and difficult process. You may need to enlist the help of an attorney.

Setback requirements mandate the number of feet between the building area and the property line. Setbacks are designed to provide adequate space between buildings for light, ventilation, access, and privacy. Most residential areas require 10 or more feet from the side property boundary to the buildable area. Setbacks for the front and back are usually much larger and depend on the size of the lot. The best way to check your setback restrictions is to review your home's survey plat. If you do not have a copy, you can request one from your local authority. To protect yourself from costly changes, do not build out of your property's approved buildable area. If you do, even if you obtain a variance permit, both current and future owners of neighboring properties can try to force you to move your addition.

An easement is a legal interest in a parcel of land that is owned by someone other than the landowner. The homeowner does not own the rights to the land use on an easement even though it is on his or her property. For example, utility companies most likely have easements on your property so that they can run sewer or power lines to your home. On most easement areas you are not allowed to place any permanent structures. In some instances sheds or fences are allowed. It is highly unlikely that an easement can be changed to accommodate an addition, particularly if pipes or wires are underground.

A coat of paint on the cabinets and a new kitchen island give this 1950s kitchen old-fashioned flavor.

before

NUMBERS TO KNOW

These measurements, developed by the National Kitchen & Bath Association, will help you design a kitchen that is efficient and comfortable for most users. Please note that the numbers are only guidelines. Your individual needs may vary. Always follow the measurements recommended by the makers of your appliances and other components.

Door entry: The opening of a doorway should be at least 34 inches wide. No entry door should interfere with appliances, nor should appliance doors interfere with one another.

Work centers: In a kitchen with three work centers (a major appliance or sink and its surrounding landing area and work area), the sum of the distances between the three should equal no more than 26 feet, with no single leg of the triangle measuring less than 4 feet or more than 9 feet. (Each leg is measured from the center front of the appliance or sink.) When the kitchen plan includes more than three primary work centers, each additional travel distance to another work center should measure no less than 4 feet and no more than 9 feet. No work triangle leg should intersect an island, peninsula, or other obstacle by more than 12 inches.

Aisles

The width of a work aisle should be at least 42 inches for one cook and at least 48 inches for multiple cooks. The width of a walkway should be at least 36 inches.

Cleanup/prep sink placement: If a kitchen has only one sink, locate it adjacent to or across from the cooking surface and refrigerator. Include a landing area at least 24 inches wide on one side of the sink and an area at least 18 inches wide on the other side.

Include a section of continuous countertop at least 36 inches wide by 24 inches deep immediately next to a sink for a primary preparation/work area. The primary dishwasher should be within 36 inches of the nearest cleanup or prep sink.

Auxiliary sink

At least 3 inches of countertop frontage should be provided on one side of the auxiliary sink and 18 inches of countertop frontage on the other side, both at the same height as the sink.

Refrigerator landing area

Include the following minimum measurements:

a. 15 inches of landing area on the handle side of the refrigerator or

b. 15 inches of landing area on each side of a side-by-side refrigerator or

c. 15 inches of landing area that is no more than 48 inches across from the front of the refrigerator or

d. 15 inches of landing area above or adjacent to any undercounter-style refrigeration appliance.

Cooking surfaces

Include a minimum of 12 inches of landing area on one side of a cooking surface and 15 inches on the other side. Allow 24 inches of clearance between the heating element and a noncombustible surface above it.

Code requirements:

At least 30 inches of clearance is required between the cooking surface and an unprotected/combustible surface above it.

If a microwave-hood combination is used above the cooking surface, the manufacturer's specifications should be followed.

Refer to manufacturers' specifications or local building codes for other considerations.

Ventilation: Provide a correctly sized, ducted ventilation system for cooking surface appliances. The recommended minimum is 150 cfm.

Microwave oven: Locate the microwave oven after considering the user's height and abilities. The ideal location for the bottom of the microwave is 3 inches below the principle user's shoulder but no more than 54 inches above the floor. If the microwave oven is

Open shelves are less costly than cabinets and increase sight lines, making a small room appear larger.

REMODELING SURVIVAL

The inconvenience of living in your home while you are remodeling is easier to handle if you're prepared. Dangling wires, exposed wall studs, and old insulation are not pretty sights, and they do not create a relaxing environment for you to come home to. Help control the chaos by working with your contractor before you start your project to develop a plan to minimize disruption.

Discuss what the contractor will do to control dust. Most contractors, at a minimum, tape plastic barriers at doorways to contain dust in the construction zone. Some may also tape off heat registers and change the furnace filters daily, especially when sanding drywall. Request that they cover the walkways and carpeted areas that lead to the construction zone with drop cloths.

Ask workers to arrive and leave at reasonable hours for your household. Understand that if you set shorter workdays, you may be lengthening the duration of the project. Noise during the work hours is out of your control, but you can let the contractor know in advance if there are any times, such as holidays or special family events, when your house will be off-limits.

The day before construction is to begin, empty the kitchen cabinets and the refrigerator and remove artwork and personal belongings from shelves and the walls. Take rugs and furnishings out of the room as well.

Set up a temporary kitchen

Move the refrigerator, coffeepot, and microwave to the dining room or finished basement. If you must shut off the water for an extended period, plan on staying somewhere else. The cost of the hotel room will be worth its convenience.

Protect the children

Kids and construction sites don't mix. Power tools, exposed wires, open stairwells, and stacks of lumber can easily cause a trip to the emergency room. When possible, keep doors to construction areas shut and locked. When that's not possible, send the kids to a friend's house or a day care center.

placed below the countertop, the oven bottom must be at least 15 inches off the finished floor. Provide at least a 15-inch-wide landing area above, below, or adjacent to the handle side of a microwave oven.

Oven: Include at least a 15-inch landing area next to or above the oven. At least a 15-inch landing area that is not more than 48 inches across from the oven is acceptable if the appliance does not open into a walkway.

Countertop space: A total of 158 inches of countertop frontage, 24 inches deep with at least 15 inches of clearance above, is needed to accommodate all uses, including landing areas, preparation and work areas, and storage.

DESIGN GALLERY
Finishing Touches

Make your kitchen redo more dynamic by incorporating a few colorful fabrics, attractive accessories, and artwork. Light your displays to accentuate their beauty and make the ambience more enticing.

1. Fabric window treatments lend softness and shape to the windows. Consider choosing styles designed for privacy and light control.

2. Accessories, such as dishware and other collectibles, introduce color.

3. Artwork brings color and pattern to walls. A niche provides an ideal place for a framed piece or sculpture.

4. Use lighting to reinforce your design statement. These fixtures emphasize the Craftsman style.

5. Update moldings around doors, windows, and the ceiling to create architectural interest.

CHAPTER 9

Resources

For more information peruse the
resources that follow.

Planning and building or remodeling a kitchen that meets your needs and includes the amenities you desire requires working through numerous steps and making a variety of decisions.

In addition to the advice in this book, seek help from the professionals in your community and from the national associations and organizations involved in residential remodeling. Names and contact information for some of these organizations are listed on the following pages. You'll also find professionals listed for some of the kitchens featured in this guide.

To help you communicate with retailers and design professionals about your project, see the glossary on page 212.

Contemporary style can be warm and calm (opposite); to discover other styles, see pages 74–115. To learn more about lighting (left), turn to page 184.

RESOURCE GUIDE

American Homeowners Foundation
6776 Little Falls Rd.
Arlington, VA 22213
703/536-7776
800/489-7776 www.americanhomeowners.org

The American Institute of Architects
1735 New York Ave. NW
Washington, DC 20006
202/626-7300
800/242-3837 www.aia.org

American Society of Interior Designers
608 Massachusetts Ave. NE
Washington, DC 20002
202/546-3480 www.asid.org

ENERGY STAR
U.S. Environmental Protection Agency
Climate Protection Partnerships Division
1200 Pennsylvania Ave. NW
Washington, DC 20460
202/343-9190
888/782-7937 www.energystar.gov

National Association of Home Builders
1201 15th St. NW
Washington, DC 20005
800/368-5242 www.nahb.org

National Association of the Remodeling Industry
780 Lee St., Suite 200
Des Plaines, IL 60016
800/611-6274 www.nari.org

National Kitchen & Bath Association
687 Willow Grove St.
Hackettstown, NJ 07840
800/843-6522 www.nkba.org

U.S. Department of Housing and Urban Development
451 Seventh St. SW
Washington, DC 20410
202/708-1112 www.hud.gov

U.S. Environmental Protection Agency
Ariel Rios Building
1200 Pennsylvania Ave. NW
Washington, DC 20460 www.epa.gov

Contributors and professionals for some
of the featured kitchens
Pages 64–71
Accessible Design
Field editor: Andrea Caughey
Photographer: Ed Gohlich
Kitchen designer: Richard Gatling, Gatling Design, Inc.
3258½ Rosecrans St., San Diego, CA 92110;
619/795-8983; www.gatlingdesign.com

Pages 88–93
Soothing Contemporary
Field editor: Missie Crawford
Photographer: Emily Followill
Interior decorator: Greg Mewbourne, Greg Mewbourne
Designs, 1903 Oxmoor Rd., Suite A, Birmingham, AL
35209; 205/871-6438

Pages 118–123
Facelift Refresher
Field editor: Susan Andrews
Photographer: Bob Greenspan
Kitchen designer: Anna Marie DeMayo, 220 Doniphan,
Liberty, MO 64068; 816/560-5054

Pages 130–135
Simple Bumpout
Photo stylist: Amber Dawn Barz, Writing and Editing Services, Inc.
Photographer: Scott Little
Architect: Mike Kastner, AIA, ASK Studio, 3716 Ingersoll Ave., Suite A, Des Moines, IA 50312; 515/277-6707; www.askstudio.com

Pages 142, 144–145
Cabinetry
Field editor: Diane Carroll
Photographer: Nancy Nolan
Kitchen designer: Andrea Cornwell, ASID
Interior designer: Andi Stephens, Kitchen Distributors, NKBA
505 W. Ash, Fayetteville, AR 72701; 479/521-1313
www.kitchendistributorsinc.com

Pages 186–187
Lighting
Field editor: Susan Andrews
Photographer: Bob Greenspan
Kitchen designer: Beverly Gilbert, Regarding Kitchens, 9980 Lakeview Ave., Lenexa, KS 66219; 913/642-6184; www.regardingkitchens.com
Interior designer: Cindy Hedenkamp

Page 188, right
Lighting
Design: Thomas Trzcinski, CMKBD, Trzcinski Design Group, 7901 Perry Highway, Pittsburgh, PA 15237; 412/369-2900
www.kitchenbathconceptspittsburgh.com
Interior design: Cynthia Rosky Designs
Photographer: Craig Thompson

GLOSSARY

Accent light Lighting designed to enhance architectural amenities or display areas.

Ambient light General overhead lighting that enables you to see from one side of the room to the other.

Backsplash Protective and decorative material adhered to the wall at the back edge of a countertop, extending the full length of the countertop.

Btu (British thermal unit) The amount of heat needed to raise 1 pound of water 1 degree Fahrenheit. Heating and cooling equipment commonly is rated by the Btus it can deliver or absorb.

Building code A local ordinance governing the manner in which a home may be constructed or modified. Most codes deal with fire and health, with sections relating to electrical, plumbing, and structural work.

Bullnose tile Also called cap tile, shaped to define an edge of a surface, such as a countertop.

Ceramic tile Made from refined clay, usually mixed with additives and water and hardened in a kiln. Can be glazed or unglazed.

Crown A contoured molding sometimes installed at the top of a wall or cabinet.

Dimmer A switch that lets you vary the intensity of illumination emitted from a light fixture.

Downlight Recessed or attached to the ceiling, a spotlight that casts light downward.

Drawer slides The metal tracks or wood cleats mounted to drawers and the inside of cabinets for suspending drawers and enabling them to open and close.

Face frame The front structure of a cabinet, made of stiles and rails; it surrounds the door panels or drawers.

Fixture (1) Any electrical device permanently attached to a home's wiring. (2) Any of several plumbing devices that provide either a supply of water or sanitary disposal of liquid or solid waste.

Fluorescent light An energy-efficient light source that uses an ionization process to produce ultraviolet radiation. This becomes visible light when it hits the coated inner surface of the bulb or tube.

Flush On the same plane as or level with the surrounding surface.

Galley A kitchen layout characterized by two parallel runs of cabinetry on opposing walls.

Glazing A protective and decorative coating that is fired onto the surface of some tiles.

Grain The direction of fibers in a piece of wood; also refers to the pattern of the fibers.

Granite A quartz-base stone with a tough, glossy appearance; granite is harder than marble.

Grout The material used to fill and seal the joints between ceramic tiles.

G-shape A U-shape kitchen configuration with the added element of a peninsula joined perpendicularly to one end of the U.

Halogen A type of incandescent light that uses metal halides in compact, highly energy-efficient bulbs, tubes, and reflectors.

Hardwood Lumber derived from deciduous trees such as oaks, maples, and walnuts.

Honed finish A satin rather than high-gloss finish achieved by removing the highly polished surface.

Hutch A two-part case piece that usually has closed storage on the bottom and open shelves on the top.

Impervious tile Tile least likely to absorb water.

Incandescent bulb A light source with an electrically charged metal filament that burns at white heat.

Indirect light Light directed toward, then reflected from, a surface such as a wall or ceiling.

Island An independent segment of cabinetry that doesn't abut any walls and is typically centrally located within the kitchen floor plan.

Laminate A hard plastic decorative veneer applied to cabinets and shelves. Can refer to a material formed by building up layers, such as flooring, or to the process of applying veneer to a surface, such as countertop.

Layout A plan showing where cabinets, appliances, and fixtures will be located.

L-shape A kitchen layout characterized by two perpendicular runs of cabinetry that form an L-shape.

Marble A hard and durable limestone characterized by varied patterns and colors of veins.

Mosaic tile Small (1- or 2-inch) vitreous tiles mounted on sheets or joined with adhesive strips.

Patina The natural finish on a wood or metal surface that results from age and polishing.

Peninsula A typically short section of cabinetry joined perpendicularly to one end of an L-shape or U-shape kitchen configuration.

Rails The horizontal members of a face frame.

Receptacle An outlet that supplies power for appliances and other plug-in devices.

Stiles The vertical members of a face frame.

Stone tile Marble, granite, limestone, and slate are some examples. Dimensioned (or gauged) stone is cut to uniform size. Hand-split (or cleft) varies in size.

Task light Lighting that illuminates a specific work or grooming area.

Toe-kick The indentation at the bottom of a floor-based cabinet. Also known as toe space.

Traffic flow The route followed to enter and exit a kitchen and move through the work core.

Trim tile Tile that is shaped to turn corners or define the edges of an installation. Includes cove, bullnose, V-cap, quarter-round, inside corner, and outside corner.

Uplight A light fixture that casts light onto the ceiling.

U-shape A kitchen layout characterized by three runs of cabinetry joined perpendicularly to form a U-shape.

Work triangle The triangle formed by drawing lines from the sink to the refrigerator to the cooktop and back to the sink.

Zones Interrelated centers, or stations, laid out to make your kitchen more organized and comfortable.

INDEX